AI SUPERPOWERS

Leveraging Artificial Intelligence for
Personal and Professional Growth

Katherine Gierszal

Kindle Direct Publishing

Copyright © 2024 Katherine Gierszal

All rights reserved

The characters and events portrayed in this book are fictitious. Any similarity to real persons, living or dead, is coincidental and not intended by the author.

No part of this book may be reproduced, or stored in a retrieval system, or transmitted in any form or by any means, electronic, mechanical, photocopying, recording, or otherwise, without express written permission of the publisher.

ISBN-13: 9798343005264

Cover design by: Art Painter
Library of Congress Control Number: 2018675309
Printed in the United States of America

I dedicate this book to my husband, Bob Gierszal, my favorite human being on the planet. He keeps me centered, grounded and on point. AI has a lot of potential, but it will never match Bob Gierszal.

"The measure of intelligence is the ability to change."
—Albert Einstein

In a world where technology is reshaping every facet of life, the power to adapt and grow is the ultimate advantage. Embracing AI is not just about learning new tools—it's about unlocking the potential within ourselves to thrive in a constantly evolving landscape.

CONTENTS

Title Page
Copyright
Dedication
Epigraph
Foreword
Introduction
Preface
Chapter 1: Understanding Artificial Intelligence　　1
Chapter 2: The Future of Work and AI　　14
Chapter 3: Unlocking AI for Personal Productivity　　30
Chapter 4: AI for Personal Development　　48
Chapter 5: AI and Emotional Intelligence　　66
Chapter 6: AI in Leadership and Decision-Making　　84
Chapter 7: AI-Powered Networking and Communication　　102
Chapter 8: AI and Creativity　　121
Chapter 9: AI for Health and Wellness　　138
Chapter 10: Ethical Considerations of AI　　154
Chapter 11: AI in Financial Growth and Investments　　173
Chapter 12: Mastering AI for Lifelong Success　　192
Epilogue　　209
Acknowledgement　　211

About The Author	213
Books By This Author	215

FOREWORD

In recent years, artificial intelligence has shifted from being a distant futuristic concept to an integral part of our daily lives. Whether we realize it or not, AI is already making decisions for us—from recommending movies on streaming platforms to managing our investments and even guiding us through personal health plans. For some, this rapid advancement feels overwhelming, while for others, it presents unprecedented opportunities. The key lies in understanding how to leverage this powerful technology to enhance both our personal and professional lives.

This book, *AI SuperPowers: Leveraging Artificial Intelligence for Personal and Professional Growth*, is a guide to doing just that. It demystifies AI, offering practical strategies for integrating AI into every aspect of life—whether you're seeking to optimize your daily routine, grow your career, or make smarter financial decisions. But beyond the practical applications, this book delves into the broader implications of AI: how it's transforming industries, shaping the future of work, and challenging us to think differently about problem-solving, leadership, and continuous learning.

When I first started exploring the potential of AI, I was struck by how it seamlessly blended with our human capabilities. It doesn't replace us; it amplifies what we're capable of. This realization inspired me to write this book—because in a world where technology is advancing faster than ever before, those who understand and embrace AI will not just survive—they will thrive.

This book isn't just for tech experts or data scientists. It's for anyone who wants to be more productive, more creative, and more forward-thinking in their approach to work and life. AI is not just for large corporations with sophisticated data systems; it's for individuals looking to unlock their own personal superpowers.

As you read through the chapters, you'll discover how AI can help you master time management, improve decision-making, and even cultivate emotional intelligence. You'll learn about AI's role in financial growth, career development, and personal well-being. And most importantly, you'll gain the confidence to embrace AI as a tool that works for you—helping you achieve your goals and navigate the complexities of our fast-changing world.

I encourage you to approach this book with curiosity and an open mind. The future is already here, and AI is at its heart. How we choose to use it will shape our lives, our careers, and the world around us. My hope is that this book will empower you to harness AI's potential and turn it into your personal superpower.

Here's to a future where AI helps us achieve extraordinary things—together.

This Foreword was created with the assistance of ChatGPT, an AI language model developed by OpenAI. The AI helped generate ideas and text, which were then edited and finalized by the author.

INTRODUCTION

Artificial intelligence (AI) is no longer a distant, futuristic concept—it's here, woven into the fabric of our daily lives, shaping the way we work, learn, and interact with the world. From the apps that help us manage our schedules and finances to the algorithms that recommend what we watch, read, and buy, AI is quietly transforming the world around us. But while its presence is undeniable, many people still struggle to understand what AI truly is and how they can harness its power for their own growth and success.

This book was born from a simple realization: AI is one of the most powerful tools of our time, and yet, it is often underutilized or misunderstood by those who stand to benefit from it the most. For years, AI has been seen as the domain of scientists, tech companies, and data analysts. But the reality is that AI's potential is vast, and its benefits can extend to anyone—no matter your field, your background, or your level of technical expertise.

What if I told you that AI could help you become more productive, more creative, and more effective in both your personal and professional life? What if AI could empower you to make better decisions, develop new skills, and unlock opportunities you hadn't even imagined? This book is designed to show you how.

Whether you're an entrepreneur looking to optimize your business, a professional aiming to stay ahead in your career, or someone simply curious about how to improve your day-to-day life, *AI SuperPowers* will guide you through practical ways to use AI to your advantage. In these pages, you'll discover how AI can help you:

- Boost productivity by automating routine tasks and optimizing your time.
- Make data-driven decisions that improve outcomes in both your personal and professional life.
- Enhance creativity and innovation by using AI as a collaborative partner.
- Improve financial management through AI-powered tools and strategies.
- Learn and adapt faster in a rapidly changing world, using AI to continuously develop new skills.

But beyond the personal benefits, this book will also explore AI's broader impact on industries, the future of work, and the ethical considerations that come with embracing this technology. AI is already reshaping the world, and those who understand how to leverage it will be the ones who thrive in the years to come.

The goal of *AI SuperPowers* is simple: to empower you with the knowledge, strategies, and mindset needed to make AI work for you. You don't need to be a tech expert to benefit from AI's potential. You just need to be open to learning, adapting, and exploring how AI can enhance your life.

As you begin this journey, I encourage you to approach AI with curiosity and a sense of possibility. Whether you're just getting started with AI or already using it in your work or personal life, there's always more to discover. The tools and strategies in this book will give you the foundation to harness AI's superpowers for lasting personal and professional growth.

The future is bright for those who embrace AI's potential. It's time to unlock your AI superpowers and take control of your future.

Katherine Gierszal

PREFACE

We live in a world where change happens at a breakneck pace. New technologies emerge almost daily, transforming industries, redefining careers, and reshaping how we live. Among all these innovations, artificial intelligence (AI) stands out as a technology with the potential to profoundly impact nearly every aspect of our lives. Yet, for many, AI feels distant—something reserved for tech experts or large corporations. I wrote this book to challenge that notion and to show you how AI can be your personal ally in achieving both personal and professional success.

When I first began exploring the world of AI, I was fascinated by its possibilities but unsure of how it could fit into my life. Like many, I saw AI as a complex, technical domain best left to scientists and engineers. However, as I delved deeper, I realized that AI is far more than an advanced tool for experts —it's a resource for everyone. From automating daily tasks to enhancing creativity and decision-making, AI has the potential to make each of us more efficient, more innovative, and more capable of achieving our goals.

This book is not a technical manual. It's a practical guide designed to help you leverage the power of AI in ways that are meaningful and accessible. Whether you're looking to boost your productivity, make smarter financial decisions, or develop new skills, AI can be the key to unlocking new levels of growth. You don't need to be a tech guru to benefit from AI—you just need the right approach and the willingness to explore its possibilities.

Throughout this book, you'll find insights and strategies that will empower you to embrace AI as a partner in your journey toward success. I'll show you how AI can help you manage your time more effectively, sharpen your decision-making, and even cultivate emotional intelligence. You'll also learn how AI is transforming industries and what that means for your career, finances, and personal growth.

But more than anything, this book is about mindset. It's about seeing AI not as a disruptive force, but as a tool for positive change. It's about adopting a proactive approach to personal and professional development in a world where AI is becoming a driving force. By the time you finish this book, I hope you'll see AI as a superpower you can harness to shape your future, achieve your ambitions, and thrive in an ever-evolving world.

As you begin this journey, I encourage you to approach AI with curiosity and openness. The future belongs to those who are ready to adapt, grow, and innovate. With AI by your side, the possibilities are endless.

Katherine Gierszal

CHAPTER 1: UNDERSTANDING ARTIFICIAL INTELLIGENCE

In 2011, IBM's Watson made headlines when it defeated the reigning champions on the TV quiz show *Jeopardy!*, outperforming human players with its ability to quickly analyze vast amounts of information. What many people didn't realize at the time was that Watson wasn't just a game-show novelty. In the years that followed, Watson's AI capabilities were deployed in healthcare, where it began helping doctors analyze medical data, diagnose diseases, and even suggest personalized treatment plans for patients. This wasn't science fiction anymore—AI was stepping into the real world and transforming how we work and live.

What if the future of personal and professional growth isn't about acquiring more knowledge but about harnessing the limitless potential of AI to make smarter, faster decisions? What if the next big leap in human achievement involves working side by side with machines that can amplify our capabilities far beyond what we thought possible?

AI is already here, and its impact is undeniable. In fact, AI is expected to add over **$15 trillion** to the global economy by 2030, with applications ranging from finance to healthcare to entertainment. It's transforming industries, creating new jobs, and reshaping how we live. Those who understand and embrace AI today will be the ones who thrive in the future.

What AI Is and Why It's Transforming Industries

What AI Is: At its core, Artificial Intelligence (AI) is the simulation of human intelligence by machines. These machines are designed to think, learn, and adapt just as humans do, but with the ability to process vast amounts of data in ways humans cannot. AI systems use algorithms and statistical models to perform tasks that typically require human intelligence, such as recognizing patterns, solving problems, and making decisions.

There are two main categories of AI:
1. **Narrow AI (Weak AI):** This form of AI is designed for a specific task or a limited range of activities. Common examples include virtual assistants like Alexa or Siri, which respond to voice commands, or recommendation algorithms used by platforms like Netflix and Spotify to suggest movies or music based on user preferences. While narrow AI can outperform humans in the specific areas it's trained in, it doesn't possess general intelligence beyond those tasks.
2. **General AI (Strong AI):** This theoretical form of AI would have the ability to understand, learn, and perform any intellectual task that a human being can do. General AI would possess broad intelligence across different domains and tasks, but it's not yet achievable with current technology. Most of today's practical AI applications fall under the narrow AI category.

Why AI Is Transforming Industries: AI is revolutionizing industries in ways that are reshaping how we live, work, and interact. Here are some key reasons why AI has become a transformative force across multiple sectors:

1. **Automation of Routine and Repetitive Tasks:**
   AI systems excel at automating mundane, repetitive tasks that humans find tedious. In industries like manufacturing, AI-powered robots can perform tasks such as assembly, packaging, and quality control with greater precision and speed than human workers. In the office, AI is being used to handle data entry, manage emails, and even schedule meetings, freeing up time for people to focus on higher-value work.
2. **Data-Driven Decision Making:**
   One of AI's most powerful capabilities is its ability to process and analyze large sets of data quickly. In fields like finance, AI algorithms can assess market trends, predict risks, and optimize investment portfolios in real-time. In healthcare, AI is being used to analyze medical images, predict patient outcomes, and recommend personalized treatment plans based on data patterns that may not be apparent to human doctors. By turning data into actionable insights, AI enables better decision-making and problem-solving.
3. **Personalization at Scale:**
   AI allows companies to deliver highly personalized experiences to millions of customers simultaneously. In retail, AI analyzes browsing and purchasing habits to recommend products tailored to individual preferences. Streaming services like Netflix and Spotify use AI to suggest content based on each user's viewing or listening history. This level of customization creates more engaging and relevant experiences for consumers, which boosts customer loyalty and satisfaction.
4. **Increased Efficiency and Cost Savings:**
   AI optimizes processes across industries, driving significant cost savings and improving operational efficiency. In logistics, AI-powered systems optimize

delivery routes, predict maintenance needs for machinery, and minimize downtime. In energy, AI is used to manage power grids more effectively, reducing waste and improving sustainability. The ability to streamline operations while reducing costs is a key reason why AI adoption is accelerating in industries worldwide.

5. **Innovation and New Opportunities:**
AI is not only improving existing industries but also creating entirely new opportunities. Autonomous vehicles are revolutionizing transportation by promising safer, self-driving cars. In creative industries, AI is being used to generate music, art, and even stories, often in collaboration with human creators. As AI continues to advance, it will likely give rise to new industries and business models that we can't yet fully imagine.

The Bottom Line: AI is transforming industries because it fundamentally changes how work is done, decisions are made, and experiences are delivered. From automating routine tasks to driving innovation, AI enables businesses to operate more efficiently, make smarter decisions, and provide better services. Those who understand and embrace AI stand to benefit the most from its disruptive potential.

A Brief History of AI Development and Its Current State

The Origins of Artificial Intelligence: The concept of AI can be traced back to ancient mythology, where tales of intelligent automatons and mechanical beings appear in various cultures. However, the modern history of AI began in the 20th century with the development of computer science and the exploration of machine intelligence.

1. **The Early Foundations (1940s–1950s):**

AI's formal beginnings can be credited to British mathematician **Alan Turing**, who, in 1950, introduced the idea that machines could simulate human intelligence. His famous paper, *"Computing Machinery and Intelligence,"* posed the provocative question, "Can machines think?" and proposed the **Turing Test** to evaluate whether a machine's behavior could be indistinguishable from that of a human. This sparked the early theoretical discussions that would shape AI.

2. **The Birth of AI as a Field (1956):**
The term *Artificial Intelligence* was coined at the **Dartmouth Conference** in 1956, where computer scientists, including **John McCarthy**, **Marvin Minsky**, and **Herbert Simon**, laid the groundwork for AI as a formal discipline. Early AI research focused on logic, symbolic reasoning, and solving algebraic equations, with the aim of creating systems that could simulate aspects of human cognition.

3. **The First AI Winter (1970s–1980s):**
After initial optimism, progress in AI slowed due to technological limitations. AI systems at the time were limited by the computing power available and the inability to process vast amounts of data efficiently. This led to the **AI Winter**, a period in which funding and interest in AI research declined.

4. **Resurgence and Machine Learning (1980s–1990s):**
AI research regained momentum in the 1980s, particularly with the development of **expert systems**, which attempted to simulate human expertise in specific fields like medicine or engineering. However, the real resurgence came with advances in **machine learning** (ML), a subset of AI focused on developing algorithms that allow machines to learn from data without being explicitly programmed. **Neural networks**, inspired by the human brain's structure, also saw renewed interest as they demonstrated the

potential for machines to learn and make decisions based on large datasets.

5. **The Age of Big Data and Deep Learning (2000s–2010s):**
The explosion of digital data in the early 21st century fueled a new era of AI. Advances in computing power, combined with access to massive datasets (termed **Big Data**), enabled AI researchers to develop more sophisticated machine learning algorithms. The breakthrough came in **deep learning**, which uses multiple layers of neural networks to process complex patterns, such as recognizing objects in images or translating languages. Companies like Google, Facebook, and Amazon invested heavily in AI research, applying these advances to products such as search engines, virtual assistants, and recommendation systems.

6. **The AI Renaissance (2010s–Present):**
The 2010s marked an AI renaissance, with rapid developments in both hardware (GPUs and TPUs) and AI algorithms, especially deep learning. Innovations in **natural language processing (NLP)**, **computer vision**, and **reinforcement learning** led to practical applications in self-driving cars, virtual personal assistants (like **Siri** and **Alexa**), and AI-generated art and music. These AI systems became capable of tasks once thought to be uniquely human, such as playing chess, Go, and even composing original pieces of music.

The Current State of AI: Today, AI is embedded in almost every aspect of modern life, from personal devices to large-scale industrial operations. Its capabilities continue to expand as algorithms become more advanced and computing resources more powerful. Here are some key features of AI's current state:

1. **Ubiquity in Everyday Life:**
   AI powers everyday tools and services that millions of people use. From Google's search engine, which uses AI to deliver personalized results, to Netflix's AI-driven content recommendations, AI has become seamlessly integrated into our digital lives. AI is also behind facial recognition systems, voice assistants, and autonomous technologies like **self-driving cars**.
2. **Natural Language Processing (NLP) Advances:**
   One of AI's most impressive current capabilities is **natural language processing**. Large language models, such as **OpenAI's GPT-4** or **Google's BERT**, have advanced the ability of machines to understand and generate human language, transforming industries such as customer service, content creation, and translation.
3. **AI in Healthcare:**
   AI's current application in healthcare is revolutionizing patient care. AI-driven tools analyze medical images to detect diseases early, predict patient outcomes, and even suggest treatment plans. **IBM's Watson** has been used to assist oncologists in making treatment recommendations, while AI-powered wearables monitor heart rates and other vital signs in real-time.
4. **AI in Business and Industry:**
   Businesses are leveraging AI to optimize operations, enhance customer experiences, and make data-driven decisions. AI algorithms in finance can predict stock trends or detect fraud, while **chatbots** and virtual assistants provide 24/7 customer support in retail. AI also powers logistics, optimizing routes for delivery services and managing inventory in real-time.
5. **Ethics and AI Governance:**
   With AI's growing influence comes the need for ethical considerations. Issues surrounding AI's role in

privacy, decision-making, and job displacement have led to increasing discussions about AI governance. Tech companies and governments are collaborating to create frameworks that ensure AI is developed and used responsibly, with a focus on fairness, transparency, and accountability.

6. **AI's Growing Role in Innovation:**
AI is not just improving existing technologies but also fostering new ones. In fields like **quantum computing** and **synthetic biology**, AI is accelerating innovation, helping scientists tackle complex problems more efficiently. AI's role in research, creativity, and invention will likely expand, unlocking new possibilities in science, engineering, and the arts.

The Bottom Line: The history of AI shows its evolution from theoretical ideas to practical, real-world applications that are transforming industries. Its current state is characterized by rapid advancements in machine learning, natural language processing, and automation, all of which are reshaping the future of work, healthcare, and everyday life. AI has come a long way since its early beginnings and shows no signs of slowing down. As we continue into the AI-driven future, understanding how it developed and where it's headed is essential for harnessing its full potential.

Why AI Matters for Personal and Professional Growth Today

Artificial Intelligence is no longer a futuristic concept—it is a reality that permeates every aspect of our daily lives. Whether you're a student, professional, entrepreneur, or leader, AI has the potential to amplify your personal and professional growth in profound ways. Understanding how to leverage AI can give you a significant advantage, helping you to become more efficient, make smarter decisions, and even unlock new opportunities. Here's why AI matters for personal and professional growth today:

1. Increased Productivity and Efficiency

AI-powered tools are designed to streamline workflows and handle repetitive tasks, freeing up time for more meaningful, creative work. Whether it's automating routine tasks like scheduling, data entry, or managing emails, AI allows individuals to focus on higher-level problem-solving and decision-making.

For example:

- AI-driven virtual assistants like **Google Assistant** or **Microsoft's Cortana** help with scheduling, setting reminders, and managing tasks.
- Tools like **Grammarly** use AI to enhance writing efficiency by catching errors and suggesting improvements, saving time on editing.
- In finance, AI-powered platforms automate processes like budgeting, invoicing, and investment tracking, allowing individuals and businesses to manage their finances more efficiently.

In a world where time is one of the most valuable resources, AI's ability to enhance productivity is a key driver of personal and professional growth.

2. Smarter Decision-Making

AI excels at analyzing vast amounts of data, identifying patterns, and generating insights that humans may overlook. This capability is invaluable in helping people and organizations make informed, data-driven decisions. In professional settings, AI provides valuable insights that guide business strategy, optimize operations, and forecast future trends.

For example:

- In business, AI-powered analytics platforms, like **Tableau** or **Power BI**, allow companies to analyze customer data, market trends, and internal metrics to

make better decisions.
- In healthcare, AI tools assist doctors by analyzing patient data to diagnose diseases more accurately and suggest personalized treatments.
- In marketing, AI algorithms assess consumer behavior and predict trends, enabling more effective advertising campaigns and product recommendations.

By leveraging AI to process and interpret data, individuals and organizations can make smarter decisions, resulting in better outcomes and long-term success.

3. Personalized Learning and Development

AI has transformed how people approach learning and self-development. Personalized learning platforms, powered by AI, offer tailored education experiences, catering to individual learning styles, pace, and preferences. Whether you're trying to acquire new skills or improve existing ones, AI-driven platforms can guide you through a customized learning journey.

For example:
- Platforms like **Coursera**, **Udemy**, and **Duolingo** use AI to recommend courses and learning paths based on your progress and areas of interest.
- **AI tutoring systems** provide real-time feedback, helping learners grasp complex concepts more quickly.
- Professional development tools like **LinkedIn Learning** analyze your career path and recommend skills or courses to help you advance in your profession.

In a world where continuous learning is vital, AI enables people to stay ahead by offering personalized, efficient ways to gain new knowledge and skills.

4. Enhanced Creativity

AI is also becoming a co-pilot in creative processes. From writing to design to music, AI is providing new ways for individuals to unleash their creative potential. AI-powered tools are capable of generating ideas, suggesting enhancements, and even collaborating with humans to create entirely new forms of art, content, or solutions.

For example:
- **OpenAI's GPT** can help writers generate ideas, draft text, and even fine-tune language for clarity and engagement.
- Design tools like **Canva** use AI to offer design suggestions, making professional-grade designs accessible to everyone, regardless of their creative background.
- AI-powered music platforms like **AIVA** help musicians compose original pieces by analyzing and suggesting musical patterns.

This intersection between AI and creativity opens up new possibilities for innovation, empowering individuals to achieve creative goals more easily and efficiently.

5. Professional Edge in a Competitive Market

In today's job market, understanding AI and how to leverage it in your profession is quickly becoming a key differentiator. Companies across all industries are looking for individuals who can navigate AI tools and integrate them into business strategies. Whether it's AI-driven data analytics, customer service chatbots, or AI in marketing, possessing AI skills can make you stand out.

For example:
- In fields like **marketing**, professionals who understand how to use AI for customer segmentation, ad targeting, and campaign optimization have a competitive edge.
- In **finance**, AI's ability to analyze market trends and automate processes gives professionals who use AI tools an advantage in delivering better insights.
- In **customer service**, AI-powered chatbots are becoming standard, making professionals with skills in conversational AI implementation highly valuable.

Being AI-literate doesn't just mean knowing about the technology; it means understanding how to apply AI to enhance professional outcomes, positioning yourself as a forward-thinking leader in your field.

6. Resilience and Adaptability

As industries evolve and jobs change due to AI and automation, individuals who embrace AI are better equipped to adapt to new roles and challenges. AI can be a catalyst for personal resilience by providing tools that help people pivot, reskill, or reinvent themselves in a fast-changing world.

For example:

- AI can help professionals identify new career paths by analyzing their existing skills and suggesting adjacent roles that are in demand.
- Entrepreneurs can use AI to identify emerging trends, helping them to stay ahead in competitive markets.
- In times of uncertainty, AI can provide insights and solutions that guide more agile, informed decision-making.

In a world where change is the only constant, AI offers individuals and businesses the flexibility and tools to thrive.

The Bottom Line: AI matters for personal and professional growth because it enhances productivity, decision-making, creativity, and adaptability. Those who embrace AI's capabilities and learn to work alongside it will gain a significant advantage in an increasingly competitive and data-driven world. Whether you are an individual looking to improve your career prospects or a business aiming for long-term success, AI is a powerful tool that can help you achieve your goals.

Artificial Intelligence is no longer a distant concept—it's a transformative technology that is reshaping industries and redefining how we live and work. From automating routine tasks to providing personalized experiences, AI is already embedded in our daily lives and is rapidly expanding its influence. Understanding AI's capabilities, its history, and its current state is the first step in recognizing how it can be leveraged to improve both personal and professional outcomes. Whether through narrow AI applications like virtual assistants or through data-driven decision-making in industries like healthcare and finance, AI is proving to be a powerful tool for enhancing efficiency, creativity, and problem-solving.

As we move forward, it's essential to not only understand what AI is but also how it will impact the future of work. As industries continue to adopt AI technologies, the workplace will evolve, creating new challenges and opportunities. Those who learn to harness AI effectively will not only survive but thrive in this new era.

In the next chapter, we'll explore how AI is reshaping the future of work. From automating tasks to creating new roles that didn't exist a decade ago, AI is driving a shift in the types of skills and adaptability needed in today's workforce. We'll examine how industries are evolving, what jobs are being impacted, and, most importantly, how you can future-proof your career in this AI-driven landscape. Understanding AI's role in the workplace will be crucial for anyone looking to remain competitive and thrive in the new world of work. Let's dive into how AI is transforming the workforce and what you can do to stay ahead of the curve.

CHAPTER 2: THE FUTURE OF WORK AND AI

It was 2018, and John's accounting firm was facing the annual tax season crunch. Every year, his team spent countless hours manually reviewing tax forms, checking for errors, and preparing filings for clients. But this year was different. The firm had implemented AI-powered tax software that could scan, analyze, and flag discrepancies in seconds. What used to take his team hours or even days was now done in minutes. As the deadlines approached, John realized something remarkable: for the first time in years, his team wasn't scrambling to meet deadlines. They were freed up to focus on offering clients strategic financial advice—something the software couldn't do. The AI didn't replace his team; it empowered them to work smarter and focus on higher-value tasks.

What if the future of work isn't about competing with AI but partnering with it? In this new era, it's not about who can work harder—it's about who can adapt faster and use AI to their advantage. As technology reshapes industries, the ability to collaborate with AI will be the key to staying ahead.

By 2025, AI is expected to displace **85 million jobs** globally but, at the same time, create **97 million new roles**, according to the World Economic Forum. The future of work is not about job loss—it's about job transformation. Those who can adapt and harness AI's power will thrive in this rapidly evolving landscape.

How AI is Reshaping the Workplace and the Skills Needed to Thrive

Artificial Intelligence is transforming the workplace in ways that were once the stuff of science fiction. From automating repetitive tasks to enhancing decision-making processes, AI is fundamentally altering the way we work. While some fear that AI will replace human workers, the reality is more complex —and more promising. Rather than simply displacing jobs, AI is shifting the types of roles available and changing the skills required to succeed. In this new world of work, the key to thriving isn't competing with AI—it's learning how to work alongside it.

1. Automation of Routine Tasks:

AI is exceptionally good at taking over repetitive, time-consuming tasks, freeing up human workers to focus on higher-level, strategic work. In sectors like manufacturing, AI-powered robots handle assembly, quality control, and packaging with far greater precision and speed than human labor. In white-collar jobs, AI tools manage tasks like data entry, scheduling, and customer service inquiries, allowing employees to focus on problem-solving and creative thinking.

However, automation doesn't stop at manual labor or administrative work. AI is also reshaping knowledge-based fields. For instance, AI-driven platforms are now assisting in legal research, financial forecasting, and even medical diagnostics, all of which were once thought to require human expertise alone. In these roles, workers are no longer simply performing routine tasks but are tasked with interpreting AI-generated insights and applying them in complex, nuanced situations.

Key takeaway:

To thrive in this environment, workers need to shift their focus from doing repetitive tasks to managing and overseeing AI-driven processes. This means developing critical thinking skills, problem-solving capabilities, and emotional intelligence to handle the work that AI cannot.

2. The Demand for New Skill Sets:

As AI continues to reshape industries, the skill sets required for success in the workplace are evolving. The future will demand a mix of **technical skills**, such as data analysis, programming, and AI tool management, and **soft skills**, such as creativity, emotional intelligence, and leadership.

- **Technical Skills:**
  Understanding how AI works and how to use AI-powered tools is quickly becoming a fundamental requirement in many jobs. Even for non-technical roles, a basic understanding of AI and data literacy is essential. Workers who can analyze AI-generated data, interpret patterns, and implement AI-driven solutions will be highly sought after. Skills in areas like coding, machine learning, and data science are particularly valuable as they enable workers to develop, manage, or collaborate with AI systems.

- **Soft Skills:**
  While AI excels at processing information and completing tasks, it struggles with the human elements of work—like empathy, creativity, and leadership. As a result, skills such as **emotional intelligence**, **adaptability**, and **collaboration** are more important than ever. These skills are essential for roles that require managing teams, providing customer support, or leading organizations through change. Additionally, creativity and innovation are becoming increasingly valuable, as humans still play a critical role in developing novel solutions that AI may not be capable of generating on its own.

Key takeaway:
Workers who combine technical proficiency with strong soft skills will be the most adaptable in the AI-driven workplace. The ability to use AI tools effectively, alongside uniquely human qualities like empathy and creativity, will make individuals indispensable.

3. AI Augmenting Human Roles:

Rather than replacing humans, AI is increasingly seen as a tool for **augmentation**—enhancing human capabilities and enabling workers to perform tasks more efficiently. For example, in healthcare, AI systems can quickly analyze medical images or predict patient outcomes, providing doctors with insights that they can then use to make informed diagnoses and treatment plans. Similarly, in marketing, AI can analyze customer data to predict trends, allowing marketing teams to create more personalized, targeted campaigns.

This concept of **collaborative intelligence**—where humans and AI systems work together—will become the norm across many industries. AI can take on the heavy lifting of data processing and routine decision-making, while human workers focus on creativity, strategic thinking, and emotional engagement. This collaborative approach not only boosts productivity but also allows businesses to innovate faster and respond to changing market dynamics.

Key takeaway:
The future of work is not about AI versus humans—it's about AI **with** humans. Workers who understand how to collaborate with AI systems to augment their capabilities will be able to achieve more and take on higher-level, value-driven roles.

4. Continuous Learning and Adaptability:

AI is evolving at a rapid pace, and this means that workers must be ready to **continuously learn and adapt** to new technologies and tools. The skills needed to thrive today may not be the same skills needed five years from now, as AI continues to advance and transform industries. This shift underscores the importance of **lifelong learning**—individuals must be willing to regularly update their skill sets and learn how to use new AI technologies as they emerge.

Fortunately, AI itself is helping to facilitate continuous learning. AI-powered learning platforms can offer personalized training programs that adapt to an individual's needs, pace, and progress, making it easier for workers to develop new skills. Additionally, companies are increasingly investing in reskilling and upskilling programs to ensure their employees remain competitive in an AI-driven world.

Key takeaway:

Adaptability and a commitment to lifelong learning will be critical for staying relevant in the future workplace. Workers who proactively seek to reskill and upskill will position themselves to thrive alongside AI.

The Bottom Line: AI is reshaping the workplace by automating routine tasks, augmenting human capabilities, and creating demand for new skill sets. To thrive in this AI-driven landscape, individuals must embrace continuous learning, develop both technical and soft skills, and collaborate effectively with AI. The future of work is not about choosing between humans and AI—it's about leveraging the strengths of both to unlock new opportunities and drive success.

Automation, Machine Learning, and Their Impact on Traditional Jobs

Automation and machine learning are two of the most significant forces driving change in today's job market. They are reshaping industries by streamlining processes, improving efficiency, and reducing the need for human involvement in routine, repetitive tasks. While these technologies offer tremendous benefits in terms of productivity and cost savings, they also bring profound changes to the workforce, particularly for traditional jobs that once relied heavily on human labor.

1. Automation's Role in Streamlining Work:

Automation involves using machines or software to perform tasks with little or no human intervention. While the concept of automation has been around for decades—think assembly lines in manufacturing—AI has taken it to a new level, allowing for the automation of more complex tasks, including those involving data analysis, decision-making, and customer interactions.

- **Physical Automation:**
  Industries like manufacturing, logistics, and agriculture have embraced physical automation through the use of robots and autonomous systems. For instance, **warehouse automation** has become increasingly common, with companies like **Amazon** using robots to sort, package, and move products, greatly reducing the need for human workers in these tasks. Similarly, in agriculture, **automated harvesters** can now handle planting, watering, and harvesting crops with greater precision and efficiency than ever before.

- **Software Automation:**
  Automation is not limited to physical tasks; **software automation** is reshaping white-collar jobs by automating administrative tasks such as data entry, invoice processing, and report generation. For example, **Robotic Process Automation (RPA)** tools allow businesses to automate routine data-handling tasks, such as payroll processing or customer service ticketing. In finance, **AI-driven algorithms** can analyze market trends and execute trades automatically, eliminating the need for human traders in many cases.

Impact on Jobs:

The increased use of automation in both physical and software tasks has led to significant job displacement in some sectors. Jobs that rely on manual labor or repetitive processes are at the greatest risk of being automated. However, while some traditional jobs are disappearing, automation is also creating new roles that involve overseeing and maintaining these automated systems. Workers in industries affected by automation may need to reskill or upskill to remain relevant.

2. The Rise of Machine Learning:

Machine learning (ML), a subset of AI, is one of the key drivers behind the rapid evolution of automation. ML allows machines to learn from data, improve their performance over time, and make decisions based on patterns they identify. This technology is particularly powerful because it enables AI systems to adapt to new information without human intervention.

- **Predictive Analytics and Decision-Making:**
  In sectors like finance, healthcare, and marketing, ML algorithms can analyze large amounts of data to make predictions and recommendations. For instance, in **finance**, ML models are used to detect fraudulent transactions by analyzing patterns of spending behavior, while in **healthcare**, machine learning tools can predict patient outcomes or identify early warning signs of diseases based on medical records.

- **AI-Powered Personalization:**
  Machine learning is also at the heart of personalization efforts in industries like retail and entertainment. Companies like **Netflix** and **Amazon** use ML algorithms to recommend products and content to users based on their browsing and purchase history. This level of personalized customer experience would be impossible to achieve manually and is a direct result of machine learning's ability to process massive amounts of data quickly and accurately.

Impact on Jobs:
As machine learning becomes more sophisticated, it is taking over roles that involve analyzing data and making predictions. Jobs that require tasks like data entry, statistical analysis, or basic decision-making are increasingly being handled by ML algorithms. However, similar to automation, machine learning is also creating demand for new roles. **Data scientists**, **machine learning engineers**, and **AI specialists** are now in high demand as companies seek professionals who can build, manage, and refine these algorithms.

3. Shifting the Job Landscape:
While automation and machine learning are transforming traditional jobs, they are also reshaping the entire job landscape by creating new roles and opportunities. The rapid rise of these technologies means that certain skills are becoming more valuable, while others are diminishing in demand. This shift is leading to a growing divide between low-skill, routine jobs and high-skill, knowledge-intensive jobs that require the ability to work with or oversee AI systems.

- **Job Displacement in Routine Roles:**
  Jobs that involve repetitive, manual, or routine tasks—whether on an assembly line or in an office—are the most at risk of being displaced by automation and machine learning. For example, **factory workers**, **cashiers**, and **clerical staff** have seen a decline in demand as machines and algorithms take over their responsibilities. This trend is likely to continue as AI technologies improve and become more widely adopted.

- **Emerging Opportunities in Tech and Innovation:**
  On the flip side, automation and machine learning are creating new jobs, particularly in the tech sector. The demand for **AI specialists**, **robotics engineers**, and **data scientists** has skyrocketed. Additionally, new roles are emerging in industries like **cybersecurity**,

where AI is used to protect businesses from digital threats, and **robotics maintenance**, where skilled workers are needed to service and repair automated systems.

- **The Importance of Reskilling and Upskilling:**
As traditional jobs are automated, the need for workers to **reskill** and **upskill** becomes more pressing. Many industries are already investing in retraining programs to help workers transition from roles that are becoming obsolete to new positions that require skills in AI, data management, and machine learning. For example, a factory worker whose job is replaced by automation might reskill to become a **robotics technician**, responsible for maintaining and programming the machines that have taken over the assembly line.

Impact on the Workforce:
While the initial reaction to automation and machine learning may be fear of job loss, the reality is that these technologies are shifting the workforce rather than eliminating it. Workers who embrace change and seek out new skills in AI and automation will find opportunities to thrive in this new landscape. Those who resist change may struggle as traditional jobs continue to be disrupted.

4. The Future of Work: Collaborative Intelligence

Despite fears that automation and machine learning will make human workers obsolete, the most likely future scenario involves **collaborative intelligence**—where humans and AI work together to achieve greater outcomes than either could alone. While AI and automation handle repetitive or data-heavy tasks, humans will focus on creativity, leadership, and tasks that require emotional intelligence and strategic thinking.

In this future of collaborative work, AI will not replace humans but will **augment** their capabilities. Workers who can effectively use AI tools to enhance their own productivity and decision-making will be the ones to lead in the evolving job market. This collaboration between human workers and AI systems will define the future of work, and the key to success will be adaptability and a willingness to embrace the change.

The Bottom Line: Automation and machine learning are fundamentally reshaping traditional jobs by automating routine tasks and creating demand for new, specialized skills. While some jobs will disappear, many new opportunities will emerge for those who are willing to reskill and embrace the future of collaborative intelligence. The workplace of tomorrow will be defined by human-AI collaboration, and those who adapt will be positioned to thrive.

Embracing AI to Future-Proof Your Career

As artificial intelligence continues to reshape industries, the workplace, and job roles, one thing is clear: embracing AI is not just an option—it's a necessity for those who want to remain relevant and competitive in the future. The most successful professionals and businesses will be those who learn to work with AI, adapt to new technologies, and continuously evolve their skill sets. Whether you're just starting your career, in mid-career, or leading a business, embracing AI is essential to future-proofing your career.

1. Develop AI Literacy
To thrive in an AI-driven world, the first step is understanding what AI is and how it works. You don't need to be a programmer or data scientist to benefit from AI, but having a foundational understanding of AI concepts will be essential. AI literacy involves knowing the basic principles behind AI, machine

learning, and data analysis, as well as understanding how AI can be applied to your specific industry or role.

- **Learn the Basics:** Start by educating yourself on key AI concepts, such as machine learning, natural language processing, and automation. There are countless free and paid resources, from online courses (such as those offered by **Coursera**, **edX**, or **Udemy**) to AI-focused podcasts, books, and articles.
- **Stay Informed:** The AI landscape is evolving rapidly, and staying informed about the latest developments is critical. Follow AI thought leaders, subscribe to AI and tech publications, and participate in webinars or conferences. This continuous learning will help you stay ahead of the curve and spot opportunities to apply AI in your field.
- **Practical Application:** Once you understand the basics of AI, think about how it applies to your job or business. Explore AI-powered tools relevant to your field, whether it's AI-based marketing platforms, customer service chatbots, or AI-driven data analytics. By learning how to use AI tools, you can immediately improve your workflow and begin integrating AI into your daily tasks.

Key takeaway:

AI literacy is the foundation of future-proofing your career. Start by building a basic understanding of AI, then look for ways to apply it in your role or industry to stay competitive.

2. Develop In-Demand Skills

In a world where AI is automating many routine tasks, developing in-demand skills that are difficult for AI to replicate is crucial. These include both **technical** and **soft skills** that complement AI and enable you to work effectively alongside it.

- **Technical Skills:** Depending on your career goals, learning technical AI-related skills can be incredibly valuable. Data science, machine learning, and AI programming are highly sought-after skills across industries. Even a basic knowledge of how to work with data, run AI models, or use AI-powered tools will make you more competitive in today's job market.

- **Soft Skills:** While AI is taking over many routine tasks, it still struggles with creativity, empathy, and complex human interaction. Developing skills like **emotional intelligence**, **leadership**, **adaptability**, and **communication** is more important than ever. These skills are uniquely human and are critical in roles where collaboration, innovation, and problem-solving are required.

For example, AI may analyze vast amounts of data to offer recommendations, but it still takes a human with strong critical thinking skills to interpret that data and make a final decision. Similarly, AI chatbots can handle basic customer service inquiries, but human agents with empathy and communication skills are still needed for complex or sensitive interactions.

Key takeaway:

Focus on developing a blend of technical and soft skills. Technical skills will help you navigate and apply AI-driven tools, while soft skills ensure that you can excel in areas where human qualities are essential.

3. Continuous Learning and Adaptability

The only constant in an AI-driven world is change. Technologies will continue to evolve, and the skills required to thrive will shift. The ability to continuously learn and adapt will be the most valuable trait for future-proofing your career.

- **Lifelong Learning:** Commit to lifelong learning by regularly updating your skills and knowledge. Online learning platforms make it easier than ever to acquire new skills at your own pace. Whether it's taking a short course in AI or machine learning, learning how to work with AI-powered tools, or improving your soft skills, investing in your personal development will

ensure that you stay relevant.
- **Adapting to New Roles:** As AI evolves, so will job roles. Be open to new opportunities and willing to pivot when necessary. Roles that don't exist today may be in high demand tomorrow. For instance, careers in **AI ethics**, **AI-human collaboration**, or **AI maintenance** are emerging as new and essential fields. Being adaptable and open to change will allow you to navigate the dynamic job market.
- **Upskilling Within Your Current Role:** If you're already established in your career, consider how you can integrate AI into your current role. Whether you're in marketing, healthcare, finance, or any other field, AI is likely already being used to some degree. Upskilling within your role—learning how to use AI tools to improve your performance—can ensure you remain valuable in your organization.

Key takeaway:
Embrace a mindset of lifelong learning and adaptability. The ability to pivot and upskill will ensure that you're always prepared for the next technological shift and that your career stays future-proof.

4. Leverage AI to Enhance Your Career

Rather than seeing AI as a threat, view it as a tool that can enhance your career and open new opportunities. By leveraging AI strategically, you can boost your productivity, creativity, and decision-making, making yourself more valuable to your employer or clients.

- **Boosting Productivity:** AI tools can automate many of the mundane tasks that take up your time. By using AI to handle routine work, you can focus on high-impact activities like strategy, innovation, and relationship-building. For example, **AI-powered scheduling tools** can handle your appointments, while **AI chatbots** can

manage customer inquiries, freeing you up to focus on more complex and rewarding tasks.
- **Enhancing Creativity:** AI isn't just for automation—it can also enhance creativity. Tools like **GPT-4** can assist with brainstorming ideas, writing content, and even helping you think outside the box. In design, AI tools like **Canva** can suggest layouts and designs, while in music, AI platforms like **AIVA** can compose original tracks based on your preferences.
- **Informed Decision-Making:** AI can help you make more informed decisions by analyzing large amounts of data and offering insights you might not have considered. For example, in finance, AI algorithms can predict market trends and suggest investment strategies. In marketing, AI can help identify customer behavior patterns and optimize campaigns for better results. Leveraging AI's data-driven insights can lead to smarter, faster decision-making.

Key takeaway:
Don't see AI as a replacement—see it as a partner that enhances your capabilities. By leveraging AI to boost your productivity, creativity, and decision-making, you'll add more value to your role and ensure your career stays relevant.

5. Network and Collaborate in the AI Space

Another critical aspect of future-proofing your career is building connections within the AI ecosystem. Networking with professionals who are experienced in AI can help you stay informed about the latest developments, find mentorship opportunities, and even open doors to new career paths.

- **Join AI Communities:** There are numerous online communities, forums, and professional groups where AI professionals share insights, ideas, and job opportunities. **LinkedIn groups**, **Reddit threads**, and **AI-focused organizations** like **AI for Good** offer platforms for collaboration and learning.

- **Collaborate on AI Projects:** If you have the opportunity, get involved in projects or initiatives that incorporate AI. Whether it's a work-related project or a side hustle, the hands-on experience will deepen your understanding of AI and its applications. Collaborating with others on AI-driven projects can also help you develop new skills and gain visibility in your field.

Key takeaway:
Networking and collaboration are key to staying ahead in an AI-driven world. Build connections in the AI space, and seek out opportunities to collaborate on AI-related projects to expand your expertise and future-proof your career.

The Bottom Line: To future-proof your career in the age of AI, you must embrace AI literacy, develop in-demand technical and soft skills, commit to lifelong learning, and leverage AI to enhance your productivity and creativity. By staying adaptable and continuously evolving alongside AI, you will not only secure your career but also unlock new opportunities in an ever-changing job market.

The future of work is here, and it is being driven by the rapid advancement of AI technologies. While some jobs are being transformed or even replaced by automation and machine learning, new opportunities are emerging for those who adapt and embrace AI as a partner in their professional lives. Rather than fearing AI, it's essential to see it as a tool that can augment human capabilities, improve efficiency, and open doors to new possibilities. Whether through automating repetitive tasks, enhancing decision-making, or creating entirely new industries, AI will continue to shape the workplace in profound ways.

Success in this evolving job market will depend on your ability to reskill, upskill, and embrace continuous learning. The key is not just in understanding how AI is transforming work, but also in learning how to work with AI to enhance your own productivity and potential. Those who adapt will find that AI doesn't eliminate opportunities—it creates them.

Now that we've explored how AI is reshaping industries and the future of work, the next step is to understand how you can use AI to your personal advantage. In the following chapter, we'll dive into the practical applications of AI tools and technologies that can help you become more productive, organized, and efficient in your daily life. Whether you're managing a business, handling a busy work schedule, or simply looking to optimize your time, AI offers powerful solutions to unlock your full potential. Let's explore how you can leverage AI to automate tasks, streamline your schedule, and boost your productivity like never before.

CHAPTER 3: UNLOCKING AI FOR PERSONAL PRODUCTIVITY

Sarah used to spend hours each week organizing her calendar, responding to emails, and managing her to-do list. As a busy marketing manager juggling multiple projects, it often felt like the administrative tasks were eating up her time, leaving little room for creative work or strategic planning. But things changed when she started using AI-powered tools. Her AI assistant now schedules meetings, prioritizes tasks based on deadlines, and even filters her emails, flagging the ones that need immediate attention. Instead of getting bogged down by minutiae, Sarah can now focus on the big picture—building campaigns, brainstorming with her team, and driving innovation. With AI by her side, her productivity has soared, and she finally feels in control of her workload.

What if you could reclaim hours of your day simply by letting AI handle the mundane? In a world where time is our most valuable asset, those who leverage AI to optimize their personal productivity will not only get more done but also free themselves to focus on what truly matters—whether that's creative work, strategic planning, or simply enjoying more downtime.

Studies show that **64% of business professionals** say they spend at least 30% of their day on administrative tasks. Yet, by integrating AI tools into their workflows, employees can reduce that time by up to **40%**, according to a report by McKinsey. Imagine what you could achieve with those extra hours.

AI Tools and Technologies that Enhance Time Management and Efficiency

In today's fast-paced world, managing time efficiently has become more critical than ever. The growing demands of work, personal life, and side projects can leave us feeling overwhelmed, but AI offers powerful tools that help streamline our daily routines. From organizing schedules to automating repetitive tasks, AI can dramatically improve time management and boost productivity. Here's a closer look at some of the AI tools and technologies that can help you reclaim your time and achieve more each day.

1. AI-Powered Virtual Assistants:

AI virtual assistants like **Google Assistant**, **Apple's Siri**, **Amazon's Alexa**, and **Microsoft's Cortana** are incredibly versatile and can handle many routine tasks that take up valuable time. These assistants can help manage your calendar, set reminders, and even answer emails based on voice commands or simple text inputs.

- **Scheduling and Calendar Management:**
  AI assistants can organize meetings, manage your calendar, and automatically schedule appointments, eliminating the back-and-forth emails and the headache of finding available time slots. Tools like **x.ai** and **Clara** go a step further by autonomously scheduling meetings and handling cancellations or rescheduling when needed.
- **Task Reminders and Alerts:**
  These assistants are excellent at setting reminders for

tasks and deadlines, ensuring you never miss a key appointment or event. For instance, **Google Assistant** integrates with your calendar and can provide real-time reminders of upcoming tasks and meetings.
- **Managing Communications:**
Some virtual assistants are equipped to handle email responses, making it easy to stay on top of communications. **Cortana** can sift through your inbox, notify you of important emails, and even generate responses based on your previous communication style.

Impact on Time Management:
By offloading repetitive tasks like scheduling, setting reminders, and managing communications to AI-powered assistants, you can focus on higher-priority activities without worrying about the administrative workload.

2. AI Task Automation Tools:

Task automation tools use AI to streamline workflows by eliminating manual, repetitive tasks. These tools can handle everything from automating social media posts to generating reports based on data. By integrating AI automation into your daily workflow, you can save countless hours of work.
- **IFTTT (If This, Then That):**
IFTTT is a popular AI tool that connects different apps and devices, allowing you to create "applets" or custom automations based on triggers. For example, you can automate tasks like saving email attachments to Google Drive, syncing your calendar events with a task management tool, or posting on social media when you upload new content to a platform.
- **Zapier:**
Zapier is another automation tool that helps you create workflows, known as "zaps," between various apps. It allows you to automate processes like moving data between apps, sending personalized emails, or creating

tasks from incoming messages. For example, you can set up a workflow that automatically adds new leads from your website into your CRM system or sends email updates when a project status changes.

- **Microsoft Power Automate:**
For more advanced automation needs, **Microsoft Power Automate** helps users automate complex workflows across different platforms, making it a valuable tool for teams that want to integrate apps like **Microsoft Office**, **Trello**, or **Slack** and automate tasks across the board.

Impact on Time Management:
By automating routine processes, these tools reduce the time spent on manual data entry, content posting, and other repetitive tasks, allowing you to focus on creative or strategic work that requires human input.

3. AI-Powered Project Management Tools:

Effective project management is a crucial element of productivity, especially for teams managing multiple projects simultaneously. AI-powered project management tools not only help streamline project timelines but also optimize workflows, predict project bottlenecks, and enhance team collaboration.

- **Trello + Butler:**
Trello, a popular project management tool, integrates with **Butler**, an AI-powered automation tool that helps you automate tasks like moving cards between lists, setting due dates, and assigning tasks based on predetermined triggers. By setting up rules, you can streamline your team's project workflows without constantly managing tasks manually.

- **Asana:**
Asana uses AI features to automate task assignments and manage project timelines. It can automatically assign tasks to team members based on workloads, predict potential delays by analyzing

task dependencies, and provide real-time updates on project progress.

- **Monday.com:**
  Monday.com offers AI-powered automation to improve team collaboration and efficiency. With AI features, teams can automate status updates, task dependencies, and communication across projects. This ensures that no task falls through the cracks, and all team members stay updated in real time.

Impact on Time Management:
AI-powered project management tools reduce the need for constant oversight and manual task updates, helping teams stay on track while minimizing the time spent managing project logistics.

4. AI-Powered Time Tracking and Productivity Tools:

One of the biggest challenges to personal productivity is knowing how and where your time is being spent. AI-powered time tracking tools help you monitor your work habits and optimize your schedule by providing insights into how you use your time. By identifying inefficiencies, these tools empower you to adjust your workflow and prioritize tasks that drive the most value.

- **RescueTime:**
  RescueTime uses AI to track your digital activity, such as time spent on different apps, websites, and projects, and provides reports that help you understand your productivity patterns. The tool helps identify distractions and suggests improvements to increase focus. For example, if you spend too much time on social media during work hours, RescueTime will notify you and offer suggestions for limiting that activity.

- **Toggl:**
  Toggl uses AI to track how you allocate your time across different projects and tasks, providing detailed

reports on where you're spending the most effort. The AI feature analyzes your time entries and suggests ways to optimize your work schedule.

- **Clockify:**
  Clockify is a time-tracking tool that uses AI to track billable hours, manage team activities, and generate productivity reports. It can analyze your time data and offer recommendations on how to allocate tasks more efficiently.

Impact on Time Management:
These tools give you a deeper understanding of how you're using your time and offer data-driven recommendations to improve your productivity. By highlighting inefficiencies and distractions, they empower you to make informed changes to your work habits.

5. AI-Driven Email Management Tools:

Email management can easily take up hours of your workday, but AI-powered email tools help you manage your inbox more efficiently by automating responses, filtering messages, and sorting emails based on priority.

- **Superhuman:**
  Superhuman is an AI-driven email app that optimizes your inbox by categorizing messages based on priority and urgency. It uses machine learning to understand your email habits and preferences, allowing it to streamline email management, suggest quick responses, and even schedule emails to be sent later.

- **Boomerang:**
  Boomerang integrates with Gmail and Microsoft Outlook to offer AI-powered email productivity features. Its **Inbox Pause** feature lets you temporarily halt incoming messages so you can focus on important tasks. Boomerang also includes an AI assistant that suggests the best time to send emails based on

recipient activity.
- **SaneBox:**
SaneBox uses AI to sort your inbox, automatically filtering out non-urgent emails and ensuring that only the most important messages land in your main inbox. It analyzes your email habits and categorizes messages into different folders, such as **SaneLater** for non-urgent items and **SaneBlackHole** for emails you never want to see again.

Impact on Time Management:
AI-powered email tools help you minimize the time spent managing and responding to emails. By automating inbox organization, they free you from the constant distractions of email, allowing you to focus on high-priority tasks.

The Bottom Line: AI tools and technologies are reshaping how we manage time and productivity. From virtual assistants to task automation and time tracking, these tools not only free us from routine, time-consuming tasks but also offer valuable insights into how we can optimize our workflows. By embracing AI-powered tools, you can drastically improve your time management, making more space for creativity, strategic thinking, and achieving your goals.

How to Use AI-Powered Apps for Task Automation, Scheduling, and Focus

AI-powered apps have revolutionized how we approach daily tasks, from automating mundane chores to helping us maintain focus and optimize schedules. These tools are designed to make life easier, allowing us to concentrate on high-value activities rather than getting bogged down by repetitive, time-consuming tasks. Here's a guide on how to effectively use AI-powered apps for task automation, scheduling, and focus, so you can enhance your productivity and make the most of your time.

1. Task Automation: Freeing Up Time for More Important

Work

One of the greatest advantages of AI-powered apps is their ability to automate repetitive tasks, freeing up time for creative work, strategic thinking, or personal activities. Here's how you can use AI-powered automation tools to simplify your workflow:

- **Zapier for Workflow Automation**:
  Zapier connects various apps and services, allowing you to automate repetitive tasks that normally require manual effort. For example, you can create workflows (called "Zaps") that automatically move data between apps. A few common automations include:
    - Automatically saving email attachments to cloud storage (like Google Drive or Dropbox).
    - Creating Trello cards or Asana tasks from incoming emails.
    - Posting to social media automatically when new content is uploaded to a blog or website.

By connecting your apps with Zapier, you eliminate the need to manually transfer information or set reminders for simple tasks, saving valuable time and effort.

- **IFTTT (If This Then That) for Custom Automations**:
  IFTTT works similarly to Zapier but allows even more personal customization. You can set up "applets" to automate tasks based on conditions, such as:
    - Automatically turning off your smartphone's Wi-Fi when you leave home and turning it back on when you return.
    - Posting the same content on multiple social media platforms simultaneously.
    - Receiving notifications when a keyword is mentioned in news headlines or social media.

These automations reduce manual effort for personal and professional tasks, enabling you to focus on more important activities.

- **AI-Powered Customer Service Automation**:

For businesses, AI tools like **Intercom** and **Drift** automate customer service by using chatbots to handle common inquiries. These AI-driven bots can:
- Answer frequently asked questions (FAQs).
- Help customers troubleshoot issues in real-time.
- Schedule calls or meetings for sales teams.

By automating basic customer interactions, these AI apps allow your team to focus on higher-level tasks, such as closing sales or nurturing client relationships.

Key takeaway: AI-powered automation apps save you from tedious, repetitive tasks. By automating workflows, you free up time for activities that require creativity and strategic thinking.

2. AI-Powered Scheduling: Streamlining Your Calendar

Scheduling meetings, appointments, and tasks can be a major time drain. AI-powered scheduling apps make it easier by automatically finding open slots, avoiding conflicts, and sending reminders. Here's how you can use AI to streamline your calendar and stay on top of your commitments:

- **x.ai for Autonomous Meeting Scheduling**:
  x.ai is an AI-powered scheduling assistant that handles the back-and-forth emails typically involved in setting up meetings. Simply cc the AI assistant (Amy or Andrew) on your email, and it will find the best time slots for the meeting based on participants' availability. Once a suitable time is found, x.ai automatically schedules the meeting, sends invites, and updates your calendar.

This eliminates the need for you to manually check everyone's availability, allowing you to focus on more important tasks instead.

- **Calendly for Seamless Appointment Scheduling**:
  Calendly uses AI to simplify the scheduling process by allowing others to book time directly on your calendar based on your preset availability. By sharing

your Calendly link, clients or colleagues can select a time that works for them, and the app handles the rest, including sending confirmation emails and reminders. Calendly integrates with tools like Google Calendar, Microsoft Outlook, and Zoom, streamlining the entire scheduling process.

- **Google Calendar's Smart Scheduling Features**:
  Google Calendar leverages AI to help you optimize your daily schedule. It can:
    - Automatically suggest meeting times based on the availability of participants.
    - Integrate with AI assistants like **Google Assistant** to schedule appointments via voice commands.
    - Provide reminders and suggest time slots for tasks that have no set deadline, helping you plan out your day efficiently.

With these AI-driven features, Google Calendar ensures that you spend less time managing your schedule and more time focusing on your goals.

Key takeaway: AI-powered scheduling apps eliminate the hassle of managing calendars, automate meeting arrangements, and help you stay organized, leaving you with more time to concentrate on high-priority tasks.

3. AI Tools for Focus: Minimizing Distractions and Maximizing Productivity

In a world filled with distractions, maintaining focus can be challenging. AI-powered tools help you stay productive by identifying distractions, managing your time, and ensuring you concentrate on the tasks that matter most.

- **RescueTime for Distraction Management**:
  RescueTime is an AI-powered time management tool that runs in the background, tracking how you spend your time on apps and websites. It provides detailed reports on your daily habits, highlights where you

lose time to distractions (such as social media or non-work-related websites), and suggests strategies for improving focus.

RescueTime's **FocusTime** feature allows you to block distracting websites during specific work periods, ensuring that you stay focused on the task at hand. Over time, the app's AI will learn your habits and offer personalized recommendations on how to improve your productivity.

- **Serene for Deep Focus Sessions**:
  Serene is an AI-powered app designed for deep focus sessions. It allows you to set daily goals and uses AI to suggest the optimal length of time for each work session, based on your previous productivity levels. It also offers:
  - Timed focus sessions, with breaks built in to maintain energy levels.
  - Website blockers to prevent distractions during focus periods.
  - A calm interface to create a distraction-free environment.

Serene is ideal for professionals who need uninterrupted time to work on complex projects or creative tasks.

- **Brain.fm for Focus-Enhancing Soundscapes**:
  Brain.fm uses AI-generated music to help you stay focused. The app's soundtracks are scientifically designed to improve concentration and block distractions. By analyzing how your brain responds to certain frequencies, Brain.fm tailors music to your specific needs, helping you enter a deep focus state more quickly.

Whether you're writing, coding, or studying, Brain.fm's AI-enhanced soundscapes are proven to boost focus and productivity.

Key takeaway: AI-powered focus tools help you eliminate distractions, manage your time effectively, and maintain concentration on important tasks, ultimately boosting productivity and allowing you to accomplish more in less time.

The Bottom Line:
AI-powered apps for task automation, scheduling, and focus are essential tools for maximizing personal productivity. By using these technologies, you can automate time-consuming tasks, streamline scheduling, and enhance focus, leaving more room for strategic thinking, creativity, and achieving your personal and professional goals.

Case Studies of Individuals Who Have Used AI to Boost Their Productivity

AI-powered tools are transforming the way people work and manage their time. From automating routine tasks to enhancing focus, AI is helping individuals across various industries maximize their productivity and free up valuable time for more creative and strategic activities. In this section, we'll explore case studies of individuals who have successfully leveraged AI to significantly boost their productivity.

1. Sarah: Marketing Manager and Time Management Enthusiast
Problem:
Sarah, a marketing manager at a fast-growing startup, struggled to balance her team's projects, client meetings, and personal tasks. She found herself spending countless hours coordinating schedules, responding to emails, and tracking the progress of multiple marketing campaigns. These administrative duties left her with little time to focus on creative work and strategic planning.
Solution:
Sarah adopted several AI-powered tools to automate her routine tasks and manage her workload more efficiently. She integrated **Calendly** for scheduling, **Trello** with **Butler** for project

management automation, and **Grammarly** for improving her email communication.

- **Calendly** took over the task of scheduling meetings, automatically coordinating with clients and colleagues based on her availability. This eliminated the constant back-and-forth emails.
- **Trello + Butler** automated her project workflows, moving tasks between boards, assigning them to team members, and setting deadlines without manual input.
- **Grammarly** helped her improve email communication by providing AI-generated suggestions, reducing the time spent editing and rewriting.

Result:
With these AI tools in place, Sarah saw a **40% reduction in time spent on administrative tasks**. She reclaimed hours of her day, which she now dedicates to brainstorming marketing strategies, developing creative campaigns, and leading team meetings. Sarah's increased focus on high-impact work has directly contributed to the company's growing success.

---

2. John: Freelance Graphic Designer Maximizing Creative Output

Problem:
As a freelance graphic designer, John found himself spending a large portion of his day on non-design tasks such as managing client communications, organizing his workload, and juggling multiple deadlines. With these responsibilities piling up, John's creativity was often stifled, and he struggled to meet project deadlines efficiently.

Solution:
John turned to AI-powered tools like **Superhuman** for email management, **Toggl** for time tracking, and **Canva's AI design assistant** to optimize his workflow and improve his productivity.

- **Superhuman** streamlined his inbox by prioritizing important client emails and automating responses to common queries, saving him significant time on email communication.
- **Toggl** provided him with insights into how he spent his time, helping him identify areas where he could work more efficiently. It also allowed him to track billable hours accurately, improving his overall project management.
- **Canva's AI design assistant** offered design suggestions, layouts, and templates, allowing him to generate visually appealing work more quickly, especially for less complex tasks.

Result:
With AI managing routine tasks, John was able to boost his creative output by **30%**. He completed projects faster without sacrificing quality, allowing him to take on more clients and increase his earnings. His improved productivity also led to better client satisfaction, as he consistently met tight deadlines while delivering high-quality work.

---

3. Lisa: Financial Analyst Using AI to Make Smarter Decisions

Problem:
Lisa, a financial analyst at a major investment firm, often spent long hours gathering and analyzing financial data from various sources. The manual effort involved in compiling reports and identifying trends was overwhelming, leaving little time for strategic analysis or forecasting.

Solution:
Lisa implemented AI-powered tools like **Power BI** for data visualization, **RPA (Robotic Process Automation)** to automate data entry, and **IBM Watson** for predictive analytics.

- **Power BI** allowed her to automatically visualize financial data, making it easier to interpret key trends and share insights with her team. The tool

- also integrated with her existing financial databases, providing real-time updates on market performance.
- **RPA** took over the time-consuming task of inputting and organizing financial data from multiple sources, freeing up Lisa's time for more complex analysis.
- **IBM Watson** helped Lisa make more accurate financial predictions by analyzing historical data and providing actionable insights on potential market movements.

Result:
With AI-powered tools, Lisa's reporting process became **50% faster**, allowing her to shift her focus to strategic financial planning and client advising. The predictive power of IBM Watson also improved the accuracy of her financial forecasts, positioning her as a more valuable asset to her firm. By automating the manual aspects of her job, Lisa was able to concentrate on high-level decision-making, contributing to her firm's growth and profitability.

---

4. James: Small Business Owner Scaling Operations with AI

Problem:
James runs a small e-commerce business and was struggling to manage customer orders, track inventory, and handle customer service requests, all while trying to grow his business. The sheer volume of tasks was overwhelming, and he felt like he couldn't focus on scaling the company because he was constantly dealing with day-to-day operations.

Solution:
James implemented several AI-powered solutions, including **Shopify's AI tools**, **Intercom** for customer support automation, and **ShipBob's AI-driven fulfillment system** to streamline operations.

- **Shopify** provided James with AI-powered insights into sales trends, automatically adjusting product pricing and inventory levels based on customer demand and historical sales data.

- **Intercom** automated customer service with AI chatbots that handled common inquiries, freeing up time for James to focus on marketing and business development.
- **ShipBob** automated the order fulfillment process, optimizing warehouse logistics and shipping processes, allowing orders to be processed and delivered more efficiently.

Result:
With AI handling operations, James was able to grow his business by **25%** in the first six months after implementation. His productivity soared as he spent less time on logistics and customer service, allowing him to focus on expanding product lines, marketing strategies, and partnerships. The seamless integration of AI into his e-commerce platform has led to a more scalable and efficient business.

---

5. Emily: Academic Researcher Optimizing Workflow with AI
Problem:
Emily, a PhD student conducting academic research, was overwhelmed by the time spent sifting through countless academic journals, extracting relevant data, and organizing her research notes. The manual process of gathering research materials was hindering her progress, leaving her little time to focus on writing and analyzing her findings.

Solution:
Emily adopted several AI-powered tools to streamline her research process, including **Zotero** for AI-driven reference management, **Scrivener** for organizing her research and writing, and **Iris.ai** for conducting AI-powered literature reviews.

- **Zotero** automatically organized and formatted her references, creating bibliographies with just a few clicks, significantly reducing the time spent on citation management.

- **Scrivener** helped her structure and manage her research notes, providing an intuitive interface that kept her work organized.
- **Iris.ai** used AI to read and analyze thousands of academic papers, identifying the most relevant articles based on her research questions and extracting key insights from the literature.

Result:
Emily's research workflow became **30% more efficient**, allowing her to focus on the actual analysis and writing. She completed her dissertation ahead of schedule, with more time to refine her arguments and polish her work. The AI tools not only saved time but also improved the overall quality of her research by providing better organization and access to relevant academic material.

The Bottom Line:
These case studies demonstrate the transformative power of AI across various industries. Whether you're managing marketing campaigns, working as a freelance designer, analyzing financial data, running a small business, or conducting academic research, AI tools can help boost productivity by automating time-consuming tasks and providing actionable insights. By embracing AI, these individuals were able to reclaim their time, focus on higher-level tasks, and ultimately achieve greater success in their careers.

AI is not just revolutionizing industries; it's also transforming how we manage our time, prioritize tasks, and focus on what matters most. By automating routine activities, streamlining schedules, and helping us maintain focus, AI tools empower us to be more productive and efficient in both personal and professional settings. Whether through AI-powered task automation, scheduling apps, or tools that help enhance focus and minimize distractions, the ability to leverage AI can drastically improve how we approach our daily responsibilities.

As AI continues to evolve, those who embrace its potential for personal productivity will find themselves ahead of the curve. With AI by your side, you can reclaim valuable time, stay organized, and increase the quality of your work—allowing you to focus on high-priority tasks that drive meaningful results.

Now that you've seen how AI can enhance productivity, it's time to explore its potential for personal growth. In the next chapter, we'll dive into how AI can be a powerful ally in your journey toward self-improvement. Whether you're looking to learn new skills, improve your emotional intelligence, or stay on top of personal goals, AI offers tailored solutions to support your growth. From personalized learning platforms to AI-driven wellness apps, we'll explore the ways AI can help you reach new heights in your personal development. Let's unlock the power of AI to take your self-growth to the next level.

CHAPTER 4: AI FOR PERSONAL DEVELOPMENT

When Rachel decided she wanted to learn a new language, she didn't have much time to commit to formal classes or even follow a strict schedule. Her work, social life, and family commitments made it difficult to find the consistency she needed. That's when she discovered AI-powered apps like **Duolingo** and **Babbel**, which tailored lessons to her daily routine. The apps tracked her progress, adapted lessons based on her strengths and weaknesses, and even sent gentle reminders to keep her on track. In a few months, she made more progress than she had with any previous attempt at learning a language. The flexibility and personalization that AI offered made a world of difference.

What if personal development didn't have to follow a rigid structure? What if AI could adapt to your unique pace, preferences, and goals, helping you achieve more in less time? In the era of AI, self-improvement no longer requires strict schedules or overwhelming dedication—it simply requires the right tools.

According to a study by McKinsey, **70% of employees say they need to continuously reskill or upskill to stay competitive in their careers**. AI-powered learning platforms, like personalized education apps, are helping people do just that. In fact, users of

AI-based learning tools report a **25% faster improvement rate** in their skills compared to traditional methods.

How AI Can Assist with Personal Growth, Learning, and Skill Acquisition

AI has revolutionized personal development by making learning more personalized, accessible, and efficient. Whether you're looking to acquire new skills for career advancement, improve your emotional intelligence, or cultivate new hobbies, AI-driven tools can tailor your growth journey to your unique needs. Here's how AI can assist with personal growth, learning, and skill acquisition.

1. Personalized Learning Paths:

One of AI's most powerful contributions to education and personal development is its ability to create customized learning paths based on an individual's preferences, goals, and current skill levels. Unlike traditional learning environments that offer a one-size-fits-all approach, AI-powered platforms adapt lessons and resources to fit the learner's pace and knowledge gaps, ensuring that each individual progresses at the rate that suits them best.

- **Duolingo and Babbel for Language Learning:**
  AI-driven language learning platforms like **Duolingo** and **Babbel** track your progress in real-time and adjust lessons based on your performance. For instance, if you struggle with certain grammar rules or vocabulary, the apps will provide additional exercises to reinforce those concepts. Similarly, they reduce the focus on areas where you show proficiency, preventing you from wasting time on content you've already mastered. This level of personalization helps learners make more efficient progress and stay motivated.

- **Coursera and Udemy for Skill Development:**
  Platforms like **Coursera** and **Udemy** use AI to

recommend courses based on your learning history, career goals, and areas of interest. The more you engage with these platforms, the better their algorithms become at suggesting courses that align with your personal and professional development needs. This creates a continuous, evolving learning experience that adapts as your goals and skills change.

Key takeaway:
AI's ability to create personalized learning paths allows individuals to focus on areas where they need improvement, making learning more efficient and less overwhelming.

2. Real-Time Feedback and Adaptive Learning:
Another key advantage of AI in personal growth is its ability to provide instant, real-time feedback. Traditional learning methods often require waiting for human feedback—whether from an instructor, peer, or manager—which can slow down the process of improvement. AI, on the other hand, analyzes your performance as you go and offers immediate feedback, helping you correct mistakes and refine your skills more quickly.

- **Grammarly for Writing Improvement:**
  Grammarly is an AI-powered tool that not only checks for grammar and spelling errors but also offers real-time suggestions to improve your writing style, tone, and clarity. Whether you're drafting an email or writing a formal document, Grammarly adapts to your writing style and provides immediate feedback, making the learning process much more interactive and immediate than traditional editing processes.
- **AI-Powered Coding Platforms:**
  For those learning how to code, platforms like **LeetCode** and **Codewars** use AI to provide real-time feedback on coding challenges, helping users correct their mistakes on the spot. These platforms adapt to the learner's skill level, offering more challenging problems as they improve and easier tasks when they

struggle. This adaptive learning approach ensures that learners are always operating within their optimal zone for growth.

Key takeaway:
AI offers real-time feedback and adapts to your learning curve, providing a dynamic and responsive learning experience that speeds up skill acquisition.

3. Gamification and Motivation:
Staying motivated during personal development can be challenging, especially when the learning process is long or complex. AI-powered apps and platforms integrate gamification techniques, such as rewards, progress tracking, and challenges, to keep learners engaged and motivated.

- **Duolingo's Gamification Approach:**
  Duolingo has successfully gamified language learning by incorporating elements like streaks, rewards, and leaderboards. Users are motivated to maintain their learning streaks and earn rewards as they complete lessons. The app uses AI to track progress and adjust difficulty levels, ensuring that users are always challenged, but not overwhelmed.
- **Habit-Tracking Apps Like Habitica:**
  Habitica is an AI-powered habit-tracking app that turns personal development into a role-playing game (RPG). Users set goals and habits, and as they complete tasks, they earn points and unlock rewards. The AI tracks their progress, offers reminders, and helps users build better habits through consistent feedback and encouragement.

Key takeaway:
AI-powered gamification keeps learners engaged by providing challenges and rewards, making the learning process feel more like a game than a chore, which boosts motivation and long-term commitment.

4. AI-Assisted Skill Acquisition for Career Development:

For professionals seeking to advance their careers, AI offers tools that can accelerate skill acquisition and ensure that individuals stay competitive in rapidly evolving industries. From personalized course recommendations to AI-driven performance assessments, professionals can now identify skill gaps and acquire new competencies faster than ever.

- **LinkedIn Learning for Career Growth:**
  LinkedIn Learning uses AI to suggest courses based on your career goals, skills, and interests. The platform analyzes your LinkedIn profile, professional network, and industry trends to recommend learning paths that are most relevant to your career development. This ensures that you're always learning skills that are in demand and can directly impact your career trajectory.
- **AI for Personal Coaching:**
  AI-driven personal coaching apps like **Replika** and **BetterUp** provide personalized development advice, helping users improve soft skills such as communication, leadership, and emotional intelligence. These tools use AI to offer customized guidance, making personal coaching accessible to a wider audience and helping professionals develop the interpersonal skills needed for career success.

Key takeaway:
AI assists in career development by offering personalized learning paths, real-time performance assessments, and skill gap analyses that ensure professionals are acquiring the most relevant skills for their industry.

5. AI for Emotional and Mental Well-Being:

Personal development goes beyond acquiring hard skills; it also includes improving emotional intelligence, mindfulness, and mental well-being. AI-powered apps are now being used to help individuals manage stress, improve focus, and cultivate healthier emotional habits, which are essential for overall personal growth.

- **Headspace and Calm for Mindfulness:**
  Headspace and **Calm** are popular AI-powered apps that provide personalized meditation and mindfulness practices. These apps use AI to tailor meditation sessions based on your mood, stress levels, and mental well-being. Over time, they adapt to your progress, ensuring that each session is aligned with your emotional needs.
- **Wysa for Emotional Well-Being:**
  Wysa is an AI-driven mental health app that offers emotional support through an AI chatbot. It helps users navigate stress, anxiety, and mental health challenges by providing real-time feedback, coping mechanisms, and personalized advice. The app also tracks your mood over time and adjusts its responses to support your well-being journey.

Key takeaway:
AI-powered mental health and mindfulness apps provide tailored emotional support and well-being practices, helping individuals improve emotional intelligence and resilience as part of their personal growth journey.

The Bottom Line:
AI is a powerful ally in personal growth, learning, and skill acquisition. From creating personalized learning paths and providing real-time feedback to gamifying the learning experience and supporting emotional well-being, AI-driven tools help individuals grow faster, stay motivated, and continuously improve. By leveraging AI, you can unlock your potential and make personal development a more efficient, engaging, and fulfilling experience.

Using AI-Driven Platforms for Continuous Education and Self-Improvement

In today's fast-paced world, the need for continuous learning and self-improvement is more critical than ever. Whether you're looking to stay competitive in your career, develop new skills, or explore personal interests, AI-driven platforms offer flexible, tailored, and efficient ways to keep learning. These platforms are transforming how we approach education, enabling personalized learning experiences that adapt to individual needs, goals, and schedules. Here's how AI-driven platforms are empowering individuals to embrace continuous education and self-improvement.

1. Personalized Learning Paths for Lifelong Education

One of the most significant advantages of AI-driven platforms is their ability to create personalized learning paths. These platforms assess your current skill level, learning style, and goals to design a curriculum that is unique to you. This ensures that you're not wasting time on material you already know or moving too fast through challenging concepts. The platform continuously adapts as you progress, keeping you on track and ensuring that your learning experience remains relevant.

- **Coursera and Udacity for Professional Development:**
  Both **Coursera** and **Udacity** use AI to recommend courses based on your career aspirations, previous learning experiences, and areas of interest. The platforms assess your progress in real-time, offering personalized course suggestions and learning paths that evolve as your skills develop. This allows you to stay ahead in fields like data science, programming, and business, with courses and certifications that align with industry demands.

- **Khan Academy for Adaptive Learning:**
  Khan Academy uses AI algorithms to create personalized learning experiences for students of all ages. Whether you're learning math, science, or history, the platform tracks your progress and tailors exercises to focus on areas where you need the most

improvement. This personalized approach ensures efficient learning and reduces frustration by providing just the right level of challenge.

Key takeaway:
AI-driven platforms personalize your learning experience, ensuring that your education is tailored to your needs and goals, making it easier to stay motivated and engaged over time.

2. Self-Paced Learning and Flexibility

One of the key challenges of traditional education systems is the rigidity of schedules and deadlines. AI-driven platforms, however, offer the flexibility of self-paced learning, allowing individuals to engage with content whenever it fits their lifestyle. This flexibility is especially valuable for working professionals, parents, or anyone juggling multiple responsibilities.

- **edX and FutureLearn for On-Demand Learning:**
  Platforms like **edX** and **FutureLearn** offer courses from top universities around the world, but with the added benefit of AI-driven customization and flexibility. Learners can progress through modules at their own pace, and the AI algorithms adapt the course content to match their learning speed. The platform's AI also tracks your engagement and recommends when to revisit specific lessons, ensuring that knowledge retention is optimized.

- **Skillshare for Creative Learning:**
  For individuals looking to develop creative skills, **Skillshare** offers AI-powered course recommendations and flexible, self-paced learning modules. Whether you're interested in graphic design, photography, or writing, the platform allows you to explore new skills at your convenience. The AI tailors recommendations based on your progress, ensuring that you're constantly challenged and engaged.

Key takeaway:

AI-powered platforms allow for self-paced learning, giving you the freedom to learn on your own schedule while still providing personalized guidance and support.

3. Continuous Feedback and Skill Assessment

One of the most significant benefits of AI in education is its ability to offer continuous feedback and skill assessments. Instead of waiting for a final grade or review, AI-powered platforms provide real-time insights into your performance. This feedback helps you understand your strengths and weaknesses as you learn, enabling faster improvements and more targeted skill development.

- **Duolingo for Language Learning:**
  Duolingo uses AI to provide continuous feedback on your language learning journey. The platform tracks your progress through various exercises and adjusts the difficulty based on your performance. As you advance, the AI highlights areas where you need improvement, offering targeted exercises to help strengthen those skills. This ongoing feedback loop helps learners retain new information more effectively and stay engaged.

- **Brilliant for Interactive Learning:**
  Brilliant is an AI-powered platform designed to help individuals develop skills in math, science, and engineering through interactive problem-solving. The AI analyzes how well you understand each concept and adjusts the difficulty level accordingly. With real-time feedback, learners can immediately see where they went wrong and receive guidance on how to improve.

Key takeaway:
AI-driven platforms offer continuous, real-time feedback, helping you make quick adjustments and progress more efficiently. This immediate insight leads to faster mastery of new skills and improved knowledge retention.

4. AI-Enhanced Peer Learning and Collaboration

While personalized learning is valuable, collaboration and peer learning also play a critical role in continuous education and self-improvement. AI-driven platforms facilitate collaboration by connecting learners with similar goals, encouraging interaction, and fostering discussions that enhance the learning experience. AI can also analyze peer feedback and group interactions to ensure everyone benefits from the exchange of ideas.

- **LinkedIn Learning for Professional Networking:**
  LinkedIn Learning not only provides AI-driven course recommendations but also connects learners with industry professionals and peers working in similar fields. The platform's AI recommends networking opportunities and suggests groups or forums where learners can engage in meaningful discussions. This integration of professional networking and learning accelerates career development by exposing individuals to new perspectives and insights.

- **Slack for Collaborative Learning Communities:**
  Many organizations and learning groups use **Slack** for AI-enhanced peer collaboration. By integrating AI bots, Slack can recommend relevant channels, content, or connections based on your interests. For instance, AI might suggest joining a coding group when you're learning a new programming language or participating in a design challenge if you're enrolled in a creative course. These AI-driven suggestions help learners collaborate with peers, share knowledge, and grow together.

Key takeaway:
AI enhances peer learning and collaboration by connecting individuals with similar interests, encouraging meaningful interactions, and providing insights into group dynamics for improved collective learning.

5. Tracking Progress and Setting Personal Learning Goals

AI-driven platforms excel at helping individuals set learning goals and track their progress over time. Whether you're aiming to master a new skill or improve in a specific area, AI can offer guidance, track your achievements, and provide reminders to help you stay on course. This tracking and goal-setting ability fosters accountability, making it easier to stay committed to long-term learning goals.

- **Coach.me for Habit Tracking and Learning Goals:**
  Coach.me uses AI to help users set personal development goals, track their progress, and receive feedback. Whether you're trying to build a new habit or master a specific skill, the platform offers AI-driven suggestions and personalized coaching to keep you on track. Users can also engage with professional coaches who use AI insights to provide tailored advice.

- **Noom for Personal Growth:**
  While **Noom** is often used for health-related goals, its AI-powered behavior tracking and goal-setting tools can be applied to various aspects of personal development. The platform helps users set realistic goals, track their progress, and stay motivated through personalized AI feedback. This approach ensures continuous growth and self-improvement, whether you're focusing on health, productivity, or emotional well-being.

Key takeaway:
AI-driven platforms help users set realistic learning goals and track their progress, fostering accountability and keeping individuals motivated as they work toward self-improvement.

The Bottom Line:

AI-driven platforms are reshaping the way individuals approach continuous education and self-improvement. By offering personalized learning paths, real-time feedback, collaborative opportunities, and progress tracking, these platforms make it easier than ever to develop new skills and achieve personal growth. Whether for career development, creative exploration, or self-betterment, AI-driven platforms provide the flexibility, support, and resources needed to embrace lifelong learning and continuous improvement.

Leveraging Personalized AI Recommendations to Optimize Learning Paths

One of the most powerful aspects of AI in personal development and education is its ability to analyze an individual's learning habits, preferences, and progress to provide personalized recommendations. These AI-driven recommendations help optimize learning paths, ensuring that learners focus on the right areas at the right time. By continuously adapting to the user's performance, AI can make learning more efficient, personalized, and goal-oriented. Here's how you can leverage personalized AI recommendations to create optimized learning paths and enhance your educational journey.

1. Tailoring Learning Content to Your Needs

AI-powered platforms are designed to understand your strengths, weaknesses, and preferences, and they use this information to deliver personalized content. Unlike traditional education systems that follow a standardized approach, AI recommendations ensure that your learning experience is tailored specifically to your needs. This means you spend less time on content you've already mastered and more time on the areas where you need improvement.

- **Coursera's Personalized Course Recommendations:** On platforms like **Coursera**, AI analyzes your past courses, interests, and performance to recommend the most relevant courses for your learning goals. For example, if you've completed an introductory data science course, the platform might suggest

more advanced courses in machine learning or AI, allowing you to continue building on your knowledge. Additionally, if the AI detects that you're struggling in certain areas, it will recommend targeted resources, such as videos or exercises, to help you improve in those areas.
- **Khan Academy's Adaptive Learning Algorithms:**
Khan Academy uses AI algorithms to track your progress in real-time and adjust the difficulty of exercises based on your performance. If you're excelling in a particular topic, the AI will suggest more challenging material to keep you engaged. Conversely, if you're struggling, the AI will recommend foundational lessons or additional practice to reinforce your understanding before moving on. This personalized approach helps you move through learning material at a pace that suits you best.

Key takeaway:
Personalized AI recommendations tailor content to your specific needs, ensuring that you spend time on the most relevant material and accelerate your learning journey.

2. Optimizing Learning Efficiency

AI-powered platforms excel at identifying learning patterns and optimizing how content is delivered. By tracking how you interact with educational material, AI can suggest the most efficient ways to learn, helping you optimize your study time and focus on what truly matters. These recommendations can include adjusting the difficulty of exercises, suggesting when to review material, or identifying knowledge gaps that need to be filled.
- **Duolingo's Smart Review Feature:**
Duolingo uses AI to track how well you retain language concepts and suggests review sessions at strategic intervals. For example, if you've mastered a set of vocabulary words but haven't used them recently,

the app will recommend revisiting those words to ensure they stay fresh in your memory. This spaced repetition method, guided by AI, helps improve long-term retention and ensures that learners spend their time effectively.

- **Brilliant's Interactive Learning Paths:**
  Brilliant, an interactive learning platform for math and science, uses AI to recommend exercises and problem-solving activities based on your progress. The AI system optimizes learning by suggesting problems that align with your current skill level, keeping you engaged without overwhelming you. As you improve, the AI continuously updates the learning path to challenge you with more complex concepts.

Key takeaway:
AI recommendations optimize learning efficiency by suggesting when to review material, identifying areas that need improvement, and adjusting the difficulty of lessons, helping you make the most of your study time.

3. Addressing Knowledge Gaps with Targeted Learning

AI's ability to analyze your performance means it can identify specific areas where you're struggling and offer targeted recommendations to close those knowledge gaps. This focused approach ensures that you don't waste time revisiting content you already understand, but instead concentrate on areas that need improvement. By addressing these gaps as they arise, you can maintain a steady learning pace without falling behind.

- **LinkedIn Learning's Skill Insights:**
  LinkedIn Learning offers personalized skill insights based on your career goals, current knowledge, and industry trends. The AI evaluates your existing skills and recommends courses or lessons that address any gaps in your knowledge. For example, if you're looking to advance in digital marketing but lack expertise in SEO, LinkedIn Learning will suggest targeted courses

on SEO optimization to ensure you're equipped with the skills necessary for growth in that field.
- **Quizlet's Custom Study Plans:**
  Quizlet uses AI to generate custom study plans based on your performance in practice quizzes and exams. The AI identifies weak areas and creates personalized flashcards and exercises to help reinforce those concepts. As you progress, the AI adjusts the study plan to ensure you're focusing on the areas where you need the most practice, rather than reviewing concepts you've already mastered.

Key takeaway:
AI-driven platforms help you address knowledge gaps by providing targeted learning recommendations, ensuring that you concentrate on the areas where you need the most improvement, allowing you to build a solid foundation for further learning.

4. Adapting to Your Learning Style
AI can adapt learning content to suit your individual learning style, whether you're a visual learner, an auditory learner, or someone who learns best through hands-on activities. By analyzing how you interact with different types of content, AI platforms adjust the format of the material to match your preferences, making learning more engaging and effective.
- **edX's Diverse Learning Formats:**
  edX offers courses in various formats, including video lectures, interactive exercises, and reading materials. The platform's AI analyzes how you interact with each format and adjusts future recommendations accordingly. If the AI notices that you retain information better through interactive exercises rather than video lectures, it will prioritize hands-on activities in your future learning path.
- **Udemy's AI-Powered Course Customization:**
  Udemy allows instructors to create courses in multiple

formats, such as lectures, quizzes, and hands-on projects. The platform's AI recommends the optimal mix of content based on how you engage with the material. For instance, if you excel in quizzes but struggle with video content, the AI may suggest more interactive lessons to enhance your learning experience.

Key takeaway:
AI adapts learning materials to suit your preferred learning style, ensuring that you engage with content in a way that maximizes your retention and enjoyment.

5. Long-Term Learning and Career Growth
AI not only optimizes short-term learning but also helps you achieve long-term goals by recommending content that aligns with your career aspirations. These recommendations are often based on industry trends, skill requirements, and your personal progress. As you advance in your learning journey, AI helps you stay on track by continuously providing relevant courses and resources that contribute to your professional growth.

- **LinkedIn Learning for Career Progression:**
  LinkedIn Learning uses AI to provide long-term recommendations that align with your career growth. The platform analyzes your job role, industry, and network connections to suggest learning paths that will enhance your skills over time. As your career progresses, the AI updates its recommendations to ensure you're developing the skills needed to stay competitive in your field.

- **Pluralsight's Skill IQ Assessments:**
  For tech professionals, **Pluralsight** offers AI-driven assessments to evaluate your proficiency in specific areas, such as software development or cloud computing. Based on your Skill IQ score, the platform recommends learning paths that address gaps in your knowledge and help you achieve your long-term

career goals. The AI continuously tracks your progress, updating its recommendations as you acquire new skills.

Key takeaway:
AI helps you stay on track with long-term learning goals by providing personalized recommendations that evolve with your career progression, ensuring that you remain competitive and continue growing.

The Bottom Line:
Leveraging personalized AI recommendations can significantly optimize your learning path, helping you focus on the right content at the right time. By tailoring lessons to your needs, offering real-time feedback, and adjusting to your learning style, AI-driven platforms make continuous education more efficient and enjoyable. Whether you're addressing knowledge gaps, optimizing your study time, or aligning learning with your career goals, AI ensures that your educational journey is personalized, relevant, and goal-oriented.

AI is revolutionizing the way we approach personal growth, learning, and self-improvement. By offering personalized learning paths, providing real-time feedback, and adapting to individual learning styles, AI-driven platforms make continuous education more accessible, efficient, and tailored to your unique needs. Whether you're striving to advance in your career, develop new skills, or pursue personal interests, AI serves as a powerful partner in helping you reach your full potential. With AI's ability to offer customized recommendations, track your progress, and address knowledge gaps, personal development has never been more engaging or effective.

As we continue to embrace AI in our growth journeys, it's clear that the benefits extend beyond just learning new skills. AI can also play a pivotal role in enhancing our emotional intelligence, helping us better understand and manage our emotions, relationships, and mental well-being.

In the next chapter, we'll explore the intersection of AI and emotional intelligence (EQ). While AI has become a valuable tool for developing technical and cognitive skills, its potential to enhance emotional awareness, empathy, and communication is equally significant. We'll dive into how AI-driven tools are helping individuals build emotional intelligence, navigate complex social interactions, and foster stronger relationships in both personal and professional contexts. Let's discover how AI is transforming not just how we think and learn, but also how we connect with ourselves and others.

CHAPTER 5: AI AND EMOTIONAL INTELLIGENCE

When Daniel was promoted to a leadership position at his tech company, he quickly realized that technical expertise alone wasn't enough. Managing a diverse team with varying emotions and communication styles was challenging, and he struggled to navigate conflict resolution, provide emotional support, and create a collaborative environment. That's when he discovered an AI-powered emotional intelligence tool, Replika, which helped him practice empathy, improve his communication skills, and understand the emotional dynamics of his team better. Over time, Daniel became more attuned to the needs of his employees, fostering a more harmonious and productive work environment. His ability to connect with others, facilitated by AI, transformed not just his leadership style, but his entire team's performance.

What if AI could help you not just learn new skills but also unlock deeper emotional awareness, empathy, and communication? In a world where emotional intelligence (EQ) is becoming as important as IQ, AI is emerging as a surprising ally in helping us navigate complex emotional landscapes.

Studies show that **90% of top performers in the workplace** have high emotional intelligence, and individuals with high EQ earn, on average, **$29,000 more annually** than their lower-

EQ counterparts. As the importance of emotional intelligence continues to rise, AI-powered tools are helping individuals develop these crucial skills faster and more effectively than ever before.

The Rise of Emotionally Intelligent AI and Its Impact on Human Interaction

As Artificial Intelligence (AI) continues to evolve, it's no longer just about processing data and performing complex calculations. Increasingly, AI is being designed to understand, interpret, and even replicate human emotions—a field known as **affective computing** or emotionally intelligent AI. These AI systems are equipped with the ability to recognize emotions through voice tone, facial expressions, and text-based interactions. This shift toward emotionally intelligent AI is having a profound impact on how we interact with technology and, in turn, with each other.

1. What is Emotionally Intelligent AI?

Emotionally intelligent AI, often referred to as **affective AI**, refers to systems that can detect, process, and respond to human emotions in real time. These AI systems use a combination of natural language processing (NLP), facial recognition, and voice analysis to gauge emotional cues. By understanding the emotional state of a user, emotionally intelligent AI can tailor its responses, offer empathy, and interact in a way that feels more human.

- **Voice Assistants with Empathy:**
  Popular AI voice assistants like **Siri**, **Alexa**, and **Google Assistant** are increasingly integrating emotionally intelligent features. For example, advancements in NLP allow these systems to recognize frustration or anger in a user's voice and adjust their tone and responses accordingly. While still in its early stages, this emotional responsiveness allows for more natural,

human-like interactions with AI, reducing frustration and improving user satisfaction.
- **AI Chatbots and Customer Service:**
Emotionally intelligent AI is transforming the customer service industry by creating chatbots that can sense customer emotions. For instance, chatbots powered by companies like **Zendesk** and **IBM Watson** can analyze the sentiment of customer messages and escalate the conversation to a human agent if they detect heightened emotions, such as anger or confusion. This allows companies to offer more personalized and empathetic support, improving the overall customer experience.

Key takeaway:
Emotionally intelligent AI is capable of understanding human emotions and responding in a way that feels natural and empathetic, paving the way for more meaningful interactions between humans and machines.

2. AI's Impact on Human Interaction

The introduction of emotionally intelligent AI into our daily lives is changing the way we communicate—not just with machines but with each other. As AI becomes more adept at recognizing and responding to emotions, it is helping to bridge emotional gaps in communication and enhancing how we relate to technology. This, in turn, influences how we connect with others in personal, professional, and customer service settings.
- **Improved Workplace Communication:**
Emotionally intelligent AI is being used in corporate environments to improve interpersonal communication and team dynamics. For example, AI platforms like **Cogito** offer real-time emotional feedback to customer service agents during phone calls, helping them adjust their tone and approach based on the caller's emotional state. This kind of AI not only improves customer satisfaction but also

helps employees develop better emotional intelligence by providing insights into how their communication affects others.

- **Enhanced Remote Collaboration:**
With the rise of remote work, emotionally intelligent AI is becoming critical in maintaining team cohesion and morale. AI tools such as **Zoom's emotion recognition features** can analyze facial expressions and voice tones during virtual meetings, helping team leaders gauge the emotional state of participants. This helps managers identify when a team member may be disengaged, stressed, or frustrated, enabling them to address emotional needs in real-time, even in a virtual setting.

- **Healthcare and Emotional Support:**
AI-driven emotional intelligence is also making strides in healthcare, particularly in providing emotional support for patients. AI-powered therapy chatbots, such as **Woebot** and **Wysa**, are designed to offer empathetic listening and cognitive behavioral therapy (CBT) techniques to individuals struggling with mental health challenges. By recognizing shifts in mood through text or voice, these AI systems can offer immediate emotional support, helping users manage anxiety, depression, or stress more effectively. For many, these AI tools offer a non-judgmental, accessible form of emotional care, particularly in situations where human interaction may be limited.

Key takeaway:
Emotionally intelligent AI is influencing how we interact in professional settings, improving communication, collaboration, and emotional support. Its presence is helping individuals build better emotional awareness and connect more deeply, even in remote or virtual environments.

3. Challenges and Ethical Considerations of Emotionally

Intelligent AI

While the rise of emotionally intelligent AI holds great promise, it also introduces several challenges and ethical concerns. These AI systems are designed to mimic human emotions, but they do not genuinely "feel" emotions, which raises questions about the authenticity and trustworthiness of interactions. Furthermore, the use of AI in emotionally sensitive areas like mental health or customer service brings up concerns around privacy, data security, and the potential for manipulation.

- **Authenticity and Trust:**
  Emotionally intelligent AI may offer empathetic responses, but can users truly trust an AI system that mimics empathy without experiencing real emotions? This lack of genuine emotional depth could lead to concerns about whether AI interactions are manipulative or inauthentic. As AI continues to evolve, developers and companies will need to ensure that these systems are transparent about their capabilities and limitations, building trust with users through clear communication.

- **Privacy and Emotional Data:**
  Emotionally intelligent AI relies on vast amounts of data to detect and respond to human emotions. This often includes highly sensitive information such as voice patterns, facial expressions, and emotional responses. The collection and analysis of such data raise privacy concerns, particularly in industries like healthcare and customer service, where emotional well-being is at stake. It is crucial for AI developers and companies to prioritize data security and ensure that users' emotional data is handled ethically and securely.

- **The Role of AI in Mental Health:**
  AI tools that offer emotional support and mental health assistance, such as therapy chatbots, bring both benefits and risks. While these tools can provide accessible support, they are not a substitute for human

therapists. Relying solely on AI for emotional support could lead to inadequate care or misinterpretation of complex emotional states. As emotionally intelligent AI becomes more prevalent in mental health care, it is essential to ensure that it complements, rather than replaces, human support systems.

Key takeaway:
Emotionally intelligent AI presents ethical challenges related to authenticity, trust, and privacy. Developers must navigate these issues carefully to ensure that AI serves as a beneficial, responsible tool in enhancing human interaction.

The Bottom Line:
The rise of emotionally intelligent AI is transforming how we interact with technology and with each other. From improving workplace communication and enhancing customer service to offering emotional support in healthcare, AI is becoming a critical tool in building empathy and emotional awareness. However, as these technologies continue to evolve, ethical considerations around trust, privacy, and the role of AI in sensitive areas must be addressed. Ultimately, emotionally intelligent AI has the potential to reshape human interaction by making technology more empathetic and responsive to our emotional needs.

How AI Can Help in Understanding and Managing Emotions

Emotional intelligence (EQ) is the ability to recognize, understand, and manage our own emotions as well as those of others. It is a crucial skill in personal and professional settings, and AI is playing an increasingly important role in helping individuals develop and enhance their emotional intelligence. AI-driven tools are now equipped to not only detect and interpret emotions but also offer strategies to manage them effectively. By leveraging AI, people can gain deeper insights into their emotional states, learn how to regulate their emotions, and improve their interpersonal relationships.

1. AI-Powered Emotion Detection and Analysis

Understanding emotions starts with accurately recognizing them, and AI has become remarkably adept at analyzing emotional cues through voice, facial expressions, text, and behavior patterns. AI-powered tools use machine learning and natural language processing (NLP) to analyze these inputs and provide feedback on a person's emotional state. This insight can be particularly helpful in identifying emotions that may be difficult to recognize, such as frustration or subtle stress.

- **Voice and Speech Analysis:**
    AI tools like **Cogito** analyze voice patterns during conversations to detect emotional changes in tone, pitch, and speed. This allows AI to determine whether a person is feeling stressed, frustrated, or calm during interactions. For example, in a customer service scenario, AI can detect signs of frustration in a caller's voice and alert the agent to adjust their approach accordingly, offering more empathetic support. These insights help individuals better understand their emotions during real-time interactions.
- **Facial Expression Recognition:**
    AI systems such as **Affectiva** and **Emotion AI** use facial recognition to analyze micro-expressions—small, involuntary facial movements that reveal emotions. These systems can interpret emotions like happiness, sadness, anger, or surprise by analyzing facial cues. While this technology is often used in customer service or marketing research, it is also being applied to help individuals understand their emotional responses during conversations or presentations, allowing them to adjust their behavior based on real-time emotional feedback.
- **Text-Based Emotion Detection:**
    Chatbots like **Replika** and **Wysa** analyze text input

to detect emotional cues based on word choice, sentence structure, and conversational tone. These AI-driven chatbots can identify when someone is feeling anxious, depressed, or stressed by analyzing how they express their emotions through text. This understanding helps guide the conversation to offer supportive responses and recommendations for managing those emotions.

Key takeaway:
AI-powered tools help individuals recognize their emotions in real-time by analyzing voice, facial expressions, and text-based cues. By providing insight into emotional states, these tools empower users to better understand their feelings and responses in different situations.

2. Emotional Regulation and Stress Management

Once emotions are identified, the next step in developing emotional intelligence is learning how to manage them. AI tools offer practical strategies for emotional regulation, providing techniques that help individuals cope with stress, anxiety, or other negative emotions. These AI-driven systems often combine cognitive behavioral therapy (CBT) methods, mindfulness practices, and personalized suggestions to guide users through moments of emotional difficulty.

- **Wysa for Emotional Resilience:**
  Wysa is an AI-powered chatbot designed to help users manage stress, anxiety, and depression. Through text-based conversations, Wysa identifies emotional triggers and provides coping strategies such as deep breathing exercises, guided meditation, or thought reframing techniques. By offering real-time support, Wysa helps users regulate their emotions and build resilience in the face of stress.

- **Headspace and Calm for Mindfulness and Emotional Balance:**
  Headspace and **Calm** are AI-powered mindfulness

apps that guide users through meditation practices aimed at reducing stress and promoting emotional balance. These apps use AI to personalize meditation sessions based on the user's emotional state, progress, and goals. By encouraging regular mindfulness practices, AI helps individuals manage emotions like anxiety, frustration, and overwhelm, improving their emotional regulation over time.

- **Mood Tracking Apps like Youper:**
  Youper uses AI to track mood fluctuations and offers personalized feedback on how to manage emotional ups and downs. By monitoring mood patterns over time, Youper provides users with actionable insights into what triggers certain emotions and how they can better regulate their emotional responses. This long-term emotional tracking helps users develop a more nuanced understanding of their emotional states and refine their emotional management strategies.

Key takeaway:
AI tools not only help users identify emotions but also provide practical strategies for emotional regulation and stress management, empowering individuals to handle difficult emotions and build emotional resilience.

3. Building Empathy and Social Awareness with AI

Emotional intelligence also involves understanding the emotions of others—empathy and social awareness are key components of EQ. AI can assist individuals in recognizing the emotional states of others and provide guidance on how to respond in a compassionate, empathetic way. Whether in personal relationships, customer interactions, or leadership roles, AI can help individuals enhance their social awareness and develop better emotional connections with others.

- **Cogito for Empathy in Customer Service:**
  Cogito is an AI tool used in customer service that provides real-time emotional intelligence feedback to

agents during phone calls. By analyzing the customer's tone of voice, speech patterns, and emotional cues, Cogito offers suggestions on how agents can adjust their communication to express more empathy. This feedback helps agents build stronger emotional connections with customers, leading to higher satisfaction and more meaningful interactions. Over time, the insights provided by Cogito can also help agents develop their own emotional intelligence, improving their interpersonal skills.

- **AI-Powered Emotional Coaching for Leaders:**
Leaders and managers are increasingly turning to AI tools for emotional coaching to improve their leadership skills. Platforms like **BetterUp** use AI to analyze communication styles and emotional interactions, offering personalized coaching on how to lead with empathy and social awareness. By tracking a leader's emotional responses and interactions with their team, AI can provide tailored feedback on how to foster stronger emotional connections, resolve conflicts, and build trust.

- **AI for Social Learning in Autism:**
AI is also being used to help individuals with autism spectrum disorder (ASD) develop emotional and social awareness. Tools like **Emotion AI** and **Mindspark** use facial recognition and emotion detection to help individuals with ASD recognize and interpret emotions in others. By offering feedback on facial expressions and body language, these tools provide valuable social learning experiences, helping individuals with ASD improve their empathy and communication skills.

Key takeaway:
AI enhances social awareness by helping individuals recognize emotions in others and offering personalized feedback on how to respond with empathy and compassion. This can lead to

stronger relationships, better communication, and improved emotional intelligence in both personal and professional settings.

4. Long-Term Emotional Growth Through AI

While AI's immediate emotional feedback can help in day-to-day situations, it also plays a crucial role in long-term emotional development. By consistently tracking emotional patterns and offering personalized insights, AI tools can help individuals reflect on their emotional growth over time, identify recurring emotional challenges, and continue refining their emotional intelligence.

- **Replika for Long-Term Emotional Support:**
  Replika is an AI companion app that engages in long-term conversations with users, helping them reflect on their thoughts, emotions, and personal growth. Over time, Replika learns more about the user's emotional patterns and provides increasingly personalized responses and recommendations for managing emotions. By offering a non-judgmental, always-available emotional support system, Replika encourages users to engage in self-reflection, ultimately leading to greater emotional awareness and growth.

- **Emotional Health Monitoring with BioBeats:**
  BioBeats is an AI-powered platform that monitors both physical and emotional health by analyzing heart rate variability, sleep patterns, and emotional states. By providing insights into how physical health impacts emotional well-being, BioBeats helps users recognize the connection between their mental and physical states. The platform offers personalized suggestions for maintaining emotional balance, helping users develop healthier habits over time and fostering long-term emotional growth.

Key takeaway:

AI tools support long-term emotional development by tracking emotional patterns, offering personalized feedback, and encouraging self-reflection. This helps users build stronger emotional intelligence over time, leading to greater resilience and emotional well-being.

The Bottom Line:
AI is proving to be a powerful ally in helping individuals understand and manage their emotions. From emotion detection and stress management to empathy-building and long-term emotional growth, AI tools offer practical, personalized strategies for developing emotional intelligence. As these technologies continue to evolve, they are providing individuals with the resources they need to navigate the complexities of emotions and build deeper, more meaningful connections with themselves and others.

Using AI for Empathy Training and Emotional Well-Being

Empathy—the ability to understand and share the feelings of others—is a critical component of emotional intelligence (EQ). It plays a pivotal role in fostering meaningful relationships, effective leadership, and compassionate customer service. However, empathy isn't a fixed trait; it's a skill that can be developed and improved with practice. AI has emerged as a valuable tool for empathy training and promoting emotional well-being, offering personalized guidance on how to cultivate empathy and create emotional balance in daily interactions. Here's how AI is being used to enhance empathy and support emotional well-being.

1. AI for Empathy Training in Professional Settings
Empathy is especially important in professional environments, where effective communication and emotional awareness can improve team dynamics, customer interactions, and leadership performance. AI-powered platforms are now being used to

train professionals in empathy, providing real-time feedback on emotional cues and offering personalized suggestions on how to respond with greater compassion and understanding.

- **Cogito for Customer Service Empathy:**
    Cogito is an AI-powered tool designed to enhance empathy in customer service settings. By analyzing the tone of a customer's voice, speech patterns, and emotional cues, Cogito provides real-time feedback to customer service agents on how they can adjust their communication style to be more empathetic. For instance, if the system detects frustration or anxiety in the customer's voice, it may prompt the agent to speak more slowly, offer reassurance, or express understanding. This immediate feedback helps agents build better emotional connections with customers, resulting in improved satisfaction and trust.
- **BetterUp for Leadership Development:**
    BetterUp uses AI to help leaders develop empathy and emotional intelligence in their management style. The platform analyzes leaders' communication patterns, team dynamics, and emotional interactions, providing personalized coaching on how to foster greater empathy within their teams. By identifying moments where leaders could have shown more empathy or understanding, BetterUp's AI-powered coaching enables managers to refine their approach to leadership, leading to more engaged and motivated teams.

Key takeaway:
AI-powered tools like Cogito and BetterUp are transforming empathy training in professional settings by providing real-time feedback and personalized coaching, helping individuals become more emotionally aware and responsive in their interactions.

2. AI for Emotional Well-Being and Mindfulness

In addition to empathy training, AI is playing an increasingly important role in promoting emotional well-being through mindfulness practices and mental health support. AI-driven apps are helping users manage stress, anxiety, and emotional imbalances by offering personalized mindfulness techniques, mood tracking, and emotional coaching. These tools are designed to promote emotional balance and well-being, helping individuals develop healthier emotional habits.

- **Headspace and Calm for Mindfulness Training:**
  Headspace and **Calm** are two of the most popular AI-driven mindfulness apps, offering meditation sessions and emotional well-being practices that are tailored to the user's specific needs. By analyzing data such as mood, stress levels, and engagement with the app, the AI suggests personalized mindfulness exercises to help users reduce stress, improve focus, and regulate their emotions. These apps provide a structured approach to mindfulness, encouraging users to practice regularly and cultivate emotional resilience over time.

- **Mood Tracking with Youper:**
  Youper is an AI-powered mood-tracking app that helps users monitor their emotional states over time and offers personalized suggestions for improving emotional well-being. By tracking daily mood fluctuations, Youper provides insights into emotional patterns and suggests exercises like gratitude journaling, breathing exercises, or cognitive behavioral therapy (CBT) techniques to promote emotional balance. The app's AI analyzes the data to provide tailored emotional support, helping users manage their well-being more effectively.

Key takeaway:
AI-driven mindfulness apps like Headspace, Calm, and Youper are helping individuals manage stress, anxiety, and emotions by offering personalized mindfulness techniques and emotional support. These tools promote emotional well-being through

regular practice and self-awareness.

3. AI for Enhancing Empathy in Personal Relationships

Empathy is not only important in professional environments but also plays a crucial role in personal relationships. AI-driven tools are now being used to help individuals better understand the emotions of their loved ones, communicate more effectively, and foster deeper emotional connections. By providing insights into emotional cues and offering suggestions on how to respond with empathy, AI helps individuals build stronger, more compassionate relationships.

- **Replika for Building Emotional Awareness:**
  Replika is an AI companion app designed to help users explore their emotions and develop emotional intelligence through long-term conversations. By engaging in text-based conversations with the AI, users can practice empathy, reflect on their feelings, and receive feedback on how they express emotions. Replika also offers personalized insights into the emotional tone of conversations, helping users become more aware of how their words might be interpreted by others. This self-awareness fosters more empathetic communication in real-life relationships.
- **Empathy in Conflict Resolution with AI-Powered Coaching:**
  AI-powered tools like **BetterHelp** offer personalized coaching on how to manage conflict in relationships through empathy. The AI analyzes communication patterns between partners, offering advice on how to navigate disagreements in a compassionate and constructive way. By providing real-time feedback on emotional cues, these AI tools help individuals stay mindful of their partner's emotional needs, leading to healthier, more empathetic conflict resolution.

Key takeaway:
AI-powered tools like Replika and BetterHelp are helping

individuals enhance empathy in personal relationships by offering personalized feedback and coaching on emotional awareness and communication. These tools promote deeper emotional connections and more compassionate interactions.

4. AI for Emotional Learning and Social Awareness

For individuals looking to develop greater social awareness and empathy, particularly in challenging social situations, AI-driven learning platforms are offering valuable support. These tools are being used to help individuals with emotional or social challenges, such as those on the autism spectrum, better recognize and respond to emotional cues in others.

- **Mindspark for Social Learning:**
  Mindspark is an AI-powered platform that helps individuals with autism spectrum disorder (ASD) improve their social and emotional intelligence. The platform uses AI to simulate social interactions, providing real-time feedback on how to recognize and interpret emotions based on facial expressions, tone of voice, and body language. This AI-driven approach helps individuals with ASD better navigate social situations, promoting greater empathy and understanding of others' emotional states.

- **AI-Enhanced Emotional Learning in Education:**
  In educational settings, AI is being used to teach emotional intelligence and empathy as part of social-emotional learning (SEL) programs. Platforms like **Hapara** use AI to analyze student interactions in collaborative projects and provide insights into how students are responding to one another emotionally. These insights are then used to guide students in building empathy, teamwork, and social awareness, helping them develop the emotional skills necessary for success in school and beyond.

Key takeaway:
AI is being used to teach emotional intelligence and social

awareness in both personal and educational contexts, helping individuals develop empathy through real-time feedback and emotional learning exercises.

The Bottom Line:
AI is revolutionizing empathy training and emotional well-being by providing personalized feedback, mindfulness techniques, and emotional support. Whether in professional settings, personal relationships, or emotional learning environments, AI helps individuals build empathy, manage emotions, and foster deeper connections with others. By integrating AI into empathy training and emotional well-being practices, individuals can enhance their emotional intelligence, leading to more compassionate, resilient, and fulfilling interactions.

Artificial intelligence is becoming a transformative tool in helping individuals develop emotional intelligence. From recognizing and managing our own emotions to building empathy and enhancing social awareness, AI-driven tools offer personalized feedback, real-time emotional insights, and practical strategies for emotional growth. Whether through empathy training in professional environments, promoting emotional well-being through mindfulness, or helping individuals build deeper connections in personal relationships, AI is elevating how we understand and navigate the emotional landscape. As AI continues to evolve, its role in shaping our emotional intelligence will expand, making emotional awareness and compassion more accessible to everyone.

However, emotional intelligence is not only essential for personal growth—it is also a critical skill for effective leadership and decision-making. Leaders who are in tune with their own emotions, as well as those of their teams, are better equipped to navigate complex challenges, inspire others, and make sound decisions. AI is increasingly playing a role in helping leaders enhance these abilities.

In the next chapter, we'll explore how AI is transforming leadership and decision-making. From data-driven insights to enhancing emotional intelligence in leadership, AI is providing powerful tools that help leaders make more informed, empathetic, and strategic decisions. We'll dive into how AI is enabling leaders to optimize team performance, manage crises, and navigate complex organizational dynamics. Let's uncover how AI is shaping the future of leadership and guiding better decision-making in today's fast-paced world.

CHAPTER 6: AI IN LEADERSHIP AND DECISION-MAKING

When Melissa became the CEO of a growing tech startup, she was faced with a complex array of decisions every day—hiring new talent, managing operations, and guiding the company's long-term strategy. She quickly realized that relying on instinct alone wasn't enough. One day, overwhelmed by data from multiple departments and struggling to make a critical business decision, she turned to an AI-powered analytics platform. The AI tool analyzed market trends, customer behavior, and operational data, providing her with actionable insights she wouldn't have identified on her own. With these insights, she confidently made a strategic decision that improved her company's product launch and saved valuable resources. AI became her trusted decision-making assistant, enabling her to focus on big-picture leadership.

What if AI could enhance not only your decision-making abilities but also your capacity to lead with confidence and foresight? In today's fast-paced world, leaders who leverage AI are gaining a competitive edge by making smarter, data-driven decisions and improving team dynamics.

According to a study by PwC, **85% of executives believe that AI will help them make better decisions** in the near future. Furthermore, companies that use AI for decision-making processes experience a **20-30% improvement in business outcomes**, highlighting AI's growing influence in leadership.

How AI Enhances Leadership by Providing Data-Driven Insights

In today's business landscape, leaders are required to make quick, informed decisions that can impact the future of their organizations. Traditional decision-making methods—often relying on intuition, past experience, and limited data—are no longer sufficient in a world of big data, fast-changing markets, and complex organizational dynamics. This is where AI comes in. By providing leaders with data-driven insights, AI enhances the decision-making process, helping leaders make more accurate, informed, and timely choices that drive success.

1. AI's Role in Collecting and Analyzing Massive Data Sets

One of AI's greatest strengths lies in its ability to process vast amounts of data in real-time, something that would be impossible for humans to do at the same speed and scale. AI can sift through massive data sets, identify patterns, and generate insights from structured and unstructured data sources—everything from customer feedback and sales figures to market trends and competitor analysis.

- **Real-Time Analytics for Business Decisions:**
  For example, AI-powered analytics platforms like **Tableau** and **Power BI** allow leaders to view real-time data visualizations that highlight important trends and potential risks. By analyzing internal and external data streams, AI can quickly uncover patterns and provide leaders with insights that are crucial for making strategic decisions. Whether it's predicting customer behavior or identifying inefficiencies in supply chains, AI offers real-time, data-driven insights that help leaders make proactive decisions instead of reactive ones.

- **Predictive Analytics for Market Trends:**
  AI tools such as **Salesforce Einstein** and **Google Analytics** go beyond historical data analysis and use **predictive analytics** to forecast future market trends, consumer preferences, and sales outcomes. For a leader making decisions about product development or market expansion, these AI-generated predictions are invaluable, allowing them to anticipate future changes in demand or shifts in the competitive landscape. This foresight enables leaders to craft more effective strategies, whether it's launching new products, entering new markets, or reallocating resources to areas of greatest potential growth.

Key takeaway:
AI enhances leadership by processing massive amounts of data in real-time, providing insights that are both deep and actionable. Leaders can use these data-driven insights to make informed decisions quickly, giving them a strategic advantage in a fast-moving business environment.

2. Improving Operational Efficiency Through Data-Driven Insights

In addition to helping leaders make strategic decisions, AI can also improve operational efficiency by identifying inefficiencies within an organization. AI tools analyze internal processes, identify bottlenecks, and recommend solutions for streamlining operations. This allows leaders to optimize resources, reduce costs, and improve productivity without compromising quality.

- **AI in Supply Chain Management:**
  Take supply chain management as an example. AI-driven platforms like **Kiva Systems** (used by Amazon) and **IBM's Watson Supply Chain** provide real-time data on inventory levels, shipping times, and supplier performance. These platforms use AI to predict potential disruptions, such as delays due to

weather or supplier issues, allowing leaders to adjust logistics plans in advance. By optimizing inventory management and reducing waste, AI helps companies maintain smooth operations while cutting down on unnecessary expenses.

- **Workforce Optimization with AI:**
  AI can also improve workforce management by analyzing employee productivity, scheduling patterns, and overall performance. Tools like **SAP SuccessFactors** and **Workday** provide leaders with insights into employee engagement and identify areas where workforce allocation can be optimized. AI can also predict when additional staffing might be needed based on historical data and upcoming demands, ensuring that leaders are better prepared to meet operational needs without overstaffing or underutilizing employees.

Key takeaway:
AI-driven insights allow leaders to optimize operational efficiency by identifying inefficiencies, predicting disruptions, and making data-backed adjustments to workflows and resource allocation.

3. Enabling Faster, More Informed Decision-Making

In leadership, time is often of the essence, and making decisions quickly can be the difference between capitalizing on opportunities or falling behind competitors. AI allows leaders to make faster decisions by automating the data collection and analysis process. Instead of spending hours or days analyzing reports, leaders can receive instant insights that are relevant to the decision at hand.

- **Automating Decision-Making with AI:**
  AI-powered tools like **IBM Watson** and **Google's BigQuery** provide decision-makers with dashboards that offer comprehensive views of the business. These tools automatically gather, analyze, and visualize data,

allowing leaders to make decisions in real-time. For example, an AI-driven dashboard might analyze sales performance across regions and suggest where to reallocate marketing budgets to maximize return on investment (ROI). By delivering actionable insights instantly, AI reduces the time it takes to make informed decisions, helping leaders respond to market changes more effectively.
- **Reducing Human Bias in Decision-Making:**
Another key benefit of AI is its ability to reduce human biases in decision-making. Human judgment is often influenced by cognitive biases—whether it's confirmation bias, recency bias, or overconfidence. AI, on the other hand, relies on data and objective analysis, offering leaders insights that are free from emotional or subconscious bias. This helps leaders make more rational, evidence-based decisions, particularly in complex situations where emotions or assumptions might cloud judgment.

Key takeaway:
AI enables faster decision-making by automating data analysis and reducing human biases. Leaders can act quickly and confidently with AI-generated insights, improving their ability to seize opportunities and mitigate risks.

4. Personalized Leadership Insights

In addition to helping leaders make decisions for the organization as a whole, AI can also provide **personalized insights** that help leaders reflect on and improve their leadership style. By analyzing feedback from team members, communication patterns, and leadership performance data, AI can offer personalized recommendations for how leaders can improve their interactions with their teams and better align their leadership approach with company goals.
- **AI-Enhanced Leadership Development:**
AI-powered platforms like **BetterUp** use data-

driven insights to help leaders assess their emotional intelligence, communication effectiveness, and leadership impact. By gathering feedback from employees and analyzing communication styles, these platforms offer tailored coaching to help leaders build stronger, more cohesive teams. For example, AI might suggest that a leader should improve their active listening skills or adjust their feedback delivery to better align with team members' needs. This personalized coaching helps leaders continuously grow and improve, making them more effective in leading their teams to success.

- **Real-Time Feedback for Leadership Improvement:**
In some organizations, AI systems provide real-time feedback on leadership interactions, offering insights during meetings or presentations. For example, AI-powered tools like **Cogito** analyze voice tone and body language in real-time, providing leaders with feedback on how their words and actions are being perceived by others. This helps leaders become more self-aware and make adjustments on the spot to foster stronger connections with their teams.

Key takeaway:
AI not only enhances decision-making but also helps leaders improve their personal leadership styles by providing data-driven insights into their communication and emotional intelligence. This feedback leads to more effective leadership and stronger team dynamics.

The Bottom Line:
AI provides leaders with data-driven insights that enhance their ability to make informed, efficient, and strategic decisions. By automating data analysis, offering predictive analytics, and delivering real-time feedback, AI helps leaders optimize operations, reduce biases, and continuously improve their leadership style. As AI continues to evolve, its role in leadership

and decision-making will only grow, empowering leaders to navigate complexity with greater confidence and precision.

Using AI to Make Better Decisions in Complex Situations

Leaders often face decision-making challenges in complex, high-stakes environments where the outcomes are uncertain and the variables are constantly changing. In these situations, human intuition and experience, while valuable, can be limited by cognitive biases, information overload, and the sheer complexity of the data involved. This is where AI excels. By processing vast amounts of information and analyzing multiple variables simultaneously, AI provides leaders with the clarity and insights needed to navigate complex situations and make more informed, confident decisions.

1. AI for Managing Uncertainty and Risk

Complex situations often involve a high degree of uncertainty, where leaders need to assess risks and make decisions with incomplete or rapidly changing information. AI helps mitigate these challenges by analyzing historical data, identifying patterns, and forecasting potential outcomes. This allows leaders to evaluate various scenarios, assess risks, and make decisions based on data rather than assumptions or guesswork.

- **Predictive Analytics for Risk Management:**
  AI-powered tools such as **RiskLens** and **Palantir** enable leaders to assess risks by analyzing data from various sources, including market trends, financial data, and operational metrics. These tools use predictive analytics to forecast potential risks and suggest mitigation strategies. For example, in a complex financial decision, AI can analyze historical stock performance, economic indicators, and market volatility to predict potential outcomes and provide risk assessments. This helps leaders weigh different options and make more informed decisions that

minimize risk while maximizing potential gains.
- **Scenario Analysis in Strategic Planning:**
AI-driven platforms like **IBM Watson** and **SAP Analytics Cloud** allow leaders to simulate multiple scenarios and evaluate the potential impact of different strategic choices. For example, in supply chain management, AI can model the effects of various disruptions—such as a natural disaster or a supplier failure—and offer recommendations on how to adjust operations to maintain continuity. By simulating different "what-if" scenarios, leaders can better understand the risks and opportunities associated with each option and make decisions that align with long-term goals while managing uncertainty effectively.

Key takeaway:
AI's predictive capabilities help leaders manage uncertainty and risk by providing data-driven insights that allow for better forecasting and scenario analysis. This enables leaders to make more informed decisions even when dealing with complex, high-stakes situations.

2. Enhancing Decision-Making in Data-Heavy Environments

One of the biggest challenges leaders face in complex situations is the overwhelming amount of data that needs to be analyzed. In sectors like finance, healthcare, and logistics, leaders are often required to make decisions based on vast amounts of information from multiple sources. AI systems are designed to process and analyze large datasets far more quickly and accurately than humans, allowing leaders to cut through the noise and focus on the most critical insights.

- **AI in Healthcare for Diagnostic Decision-Making:**
In healthcare, for instance, medical professionals are often tasked with making life-or-death decisions based on complex patient data, medical records, and research findings. AI-driven diagnostic tools like **IBM**

Watson Health and **Aidoc** can analyze patient data—including symptoms, medical history, and diagnostic images—to provide doctors with evidence-based recommendations. These AI systems rapidly analyze thousands of medical studies, cross-referencing the data to offer diagnostic suggestions and treatment plans. This not only reduces the burden of data analysis on healthcare professionals but also helps them make more accurate decisions in complex, high-pressure situations.

- **AI for Financial Decision-Making:**
In the finance sector, leaders are often required to make decisions based on market trends, financial reports, and economic indicators. AI-powered platforms like **Kensho** and **Bloomberg's AI tools** allow financial leaders to analyze massive datasets from the global economy, stock markets, and company performance reports. These platforms use machine learning algorithms to detect patterns and predict market shifts, providing leaders with data-driven insights that help them make better investment and strategic decisions in complex financial environments.

Key takeaway:
AI helps leaders navigate data-heavy environments by quickly analyzing large amounts of information and highlighting the most important insights. This enhances decision-making in complex industries where accurate, data-driven decisions are critical.

3. Improving Decision Speed Without Sacrificing Accuracy

In many complex situations, the speed of decision-making is just as important as the decision itself. Delaying action can result in missed opportunities, increased risks, or further complications. However, making quick decisions without adequate analysis can lead to poor outcomes. AI offers a solution by providing leaders with real-time insights and automating parts of the decision-making process, allowing for faster yet well-informed decisions.

- **AI in Crisis Management:**
  During crises, whether in business, healthcare, or public safety, leaders often need to make quick decisions with limited time and information. AI-powered tools like **Black Swan Technologies** and **One Concern** are designed to assist in crisis management by analyzing real-time data to predict the impact of events such as natural disasters, cybersecurity breaches, or operational failures. These tools provide leaders with real-time insights into the severity of the situation, possible outcomes, and recommended actions. This enables leaders to respond rapidly while ensuring that their decisions are based on the best available data.

- **Real-Time AI Decision Support in Retail:**
  In the fast-paced retail industry, leaders need to make quick decisions about inventory, pricing, and customer experience to stay competitive. AI systems like **Blue Yonder** and **Dynamic Yield** analyze real-time sales data, customer behavior, and market trends to provide instant recommendations on optimizing inventory levels, adjusting pricing strategies, or personalizing customer experiences. These AI-driven insights enable leaders to make fast, data-backed decisions without sacrificing accuracy, ensuring that they can respond to changing market conditions and customer demands.

Key takeaway:
AI allows leaders to make faster decisions in complex situations by providing real-time insights and automating parts of the decision-making process. This enables leaders to act quickly while maintaining accuracy and confidence in their decisions.

4. Reducing Cognitive Bias in Complex Decision-Making

Human decision-making is often influenced by cognitive biases

—subconscious tendencies that can cloud judgment and lead to irrational or less-than-optimal decisions. In complex situations, where there are many variables to consider, these biases can result in poor outcomes. AI, however, relies on objective data analysis, helping to reduce the influence of cognitive biases and offering a more rational basis for decision-making.

- **AI for Reducing Bias in Hiring Decisions:**
  In talent acquisition, for example, human biases can sometimes affect hiring decisions, leading to unfair or suboptimal outcomes. AI-driven recruitment tools like **HireVue** and **Pymetrics** analyze candidate profiles, skills, and behavioral data without being influenced by factors like gender, ethnicity, or background. These tools help leaders make more objective decisions about whom to hire based on data-driven assessments rather than unconscious biases, leading to better talent acquisition in complex hiring scenarios.
- **AI in Financial Risk Assessments:**
  In finance, AI-powered risk assessment platforms like **Zest AI** help reduce bias by using machine learning models to analyze creditworthiness without relying on traditional metrics that may be influenced by bias, such as credit scores or demographic information. These AI models use alternative data sources to assess an individual's or company's risk profile more objectively, ensuring that financial leaders make decisions based on data rather than biased assumptions.

Key takeaway:
AI reduces the impact of cognitive biases in decision-making by relying on objective data and analysis. This helps leaders make more rational, unbiased decisions in complex situations where human judgment might be clouded by personal or subconscious biases.

The Bottom Line:

AI enhances leadership in complex situations by managing uncertainty, analyzing large datasets, providing real-time insights, and reducing cognitive biases. Leaders who leverage AI for decision-making can navigate complexity more effectively, make faster and more accurate decisions, and ultimately improve outcomes for their organizations. In an increasingly complex and fast-moving world, AI is becoming an indispensable tool for leaders facing high-stakes, multi-variable challenges.

Balancing Human Intuition with AI Recommendations for Optimal Outcomes

As AI becomes an increasingly valuable tool in decision-making, one of the most important challenges for leaders is finding the right balance between leveraging AI-generated insights and relying on human intuition. While AI excels at processing data, identifying patterns, and offering predictions, it lacks the emotional intelligence, context, and creativity that human intuition provides. The key to making the best possible decisions lies in combining the strengths of both AI and human intuition, ensuring that decisions are informed by data but also guided by experience, empathy, and judgment.

1. The Strengths of AI in Data-Driven Decision-Making
AI's primary strength lies in its ability to process vast amounts of data and identify patterns that might be missed by human analysis. By providing real-time insights, predictive analytics, and objective recommendations, AI can significantly improve decision accuracy, especially in data-heavy and complex environments. However, AI recommendations are only as good as the data they are based on, and they often lack the context or nuance needed for certain types of decisions.

- **AI as an Analytical Tool:**
  AI-powered tools such as **Google's BigQuery** and **Tableau** analyze massive datasets in real-time,

providing decision-makers with insights that would take humans days or even weeks to uncover. AI excels at identifying trends, predicting future outcomes, and offering actionable recommendations based on data. For instance, AI can analyze consumer behavior data to recommend changes in marketing strategy or predict market demand for a new product based on historical trends. This data-driven approach ensures that decisions are based on factual, objective analysis rather than guesswork.

- **Enhancing Decision-Making with Predictive Analytics:**
Predictive analytics tools like **Salesforce Einstein** and **IBM Watson** provide leaders with foresight by analyzing historical data and predicting future scenarios. These tools help leaders anticipate challenges, identify opportunities, and make proactive decisions. For example, AI might predict supply chain disruptions or forecast a shift in customer demand, allowing leaders to make adjustments before problems arise. This ability to see what's coming next gives leaders a strategic advantage in planning for the future.

Key takeaway:
AI's strength lies in its ability to analyze vast amounts of data, offering leaders accurate, data-driven recommendations. These insights are critical in complex environments where data plays a central role in decision-making.

2. The Value of Human Intuition in Decision-Making

While AI is excellent at analyzing data, it lacks the emotional intelligence, creativity, and context that humans bring to decision-making. Human intuition is shaped by experience, culture, empathy, and the ability to interpret situations that are not easily quantified by data. Leaders must often rely on intuition to make decisions in areas where data is incomplete,

ambiguous, or simply doesn't tell the whole story.
- **Context and Nuance in Human Intuition:**
  Human leaders can apply their intuition in situations where AI falls short—particularly when making decisions that involve complex human dynamics, such as team morale, customer relationships, or ethical considerations. For example, an AI tool might recommend cutting costs by automating a process, but a leader might sense that implementing this change too quickly could damage team morale or disrupt company culture. In such cases, human intuition helps balance short-term efficiencies with long-term cultural or interpersonal factors.
- **Creativity and Innovation Through Human Judgment:**
  AI can process existing data, but it often lacks the ability to think creatively or innovate in the way humans can. Leaders with strong intuition can identify opportunities that don't yet exist in the data, drawing on their vision, experience, and willingness to take calculated risks. For instance, Steve Jobs' decision to launch the iPhone, a product that revolutionized the tech industry, was driven by intuition and a sense of what consumers would want, despite the lack of data at the time to support such a bold move.

Key takeaway:
Human intuition provides the emotional intelligence, creativity, and context necessary to make decisions that go beyond data analysis. Leaders must trust their instincts when the situation calls for empathy, ethical judgment, or innovative thinking.

3. Striking the Balance: Human-AI Collaboration

The most effective leaders are those who know when to rely on AI for data-driven insights and when to trust their own intuition to guide decisions. By striking the right balance between human intuition and AI recommendations, leaders can achieve optimal outcomes. This balance allows AI to handle the heavy lifting of data analysis, while human leaders focus on interpreting the insights and applying their judgment to make the final call.

- **Using AI as a Decision Support Tool:**
  AI should be seen as a decision support tool rather than a decision-making replacement. For instance, AI can offer a range of recommendations based on data analysis, but it's up to the leader to evaluate those recommendations in light of the broader context and make the final decision. A leader might weigh AI-driven insights with their knowledge of company culture, market conditions, or personal experience to arrive at a well-rounded decision.

- **When to Trust Intuition Over AI:**
  There are times when human intuition should take precedence over AI recommendations. In situations where emotional intelligence is critical—such as resolving a conflict between team members, navigating a sensitive customer interaction, or making ethical decisions—human judgment is often more reliable than AI's data-driven logic. Leaders who are attuned to the nuances of human emotions and motivations can make decisions that foster trust, collaboration, and long-term success.

- **Combining AI and Intuition in Complex Decisions:**
  In more complex decision-making scenarios, leaders can combine AI's data-driven insights with their intuition to achieve the best results. For example, an AI tool might recommend entering a new market based on data trends, but the leader's intuition might guide them to consider cultural differences, political risks, or the readiness of their team to execute the expansion. In this case, the leader uses both AI's data analysis and their intuition to make a more informed, balanced decision.

Key takeaway:
Leaders achieve optimal decision-making outcomes when they strike a balance between AI's data-driven insights and their own intuition. AI should support, not replace, human judgment, and the best decisions come from combining the strengths of both.

4. Building Confidence in Human-AI Collaboration

As AI becomes more integrated into decision-making processes, leaders must develop confidence in how to use AI effectively alongside their own intuition. This involves building trust in AI's capabilities while also knowing when to rely on personal judgment. Leaders who master this balance will be better equipped to make decisions that drive innovation, solve complex problems, and create lasting success for their organizations.

- **Trusting AI's Insights While Retaining Control:**
  To build confidence in AI, leaders must develop an understanding of how AI systems work, what data they analyze, and how they arrive at recommendations. By becoming familiar with the strengths and limitations of AI tools, leaders can make informed decisions about when to trust AI and when to lean on their own judgment. This trust-building process enables leaders to confidently use AI as a partner in decision-making without feeling that they are surrendering control.

- **Developing Intuition Through AI Insights:**
  Interestingly, AI can also help leaders refine their intuition by providing insights that challenge their assumptions or offer new perspectives. Over time, as leaders become more accustomed to analyzing data alongside AI, their decision-making intuition becomes sharper and more informed by the facts. This collaboration between AI and intuition helps

leaders make decisions that are both data-backed and emotionally intelligent.

Key takeaway:

Leaders who build trust in AI and learn to integrate it with their intuition will be better equipped to make well-rounded, confident decisions. This collaboration between AI and human judgment creates a more effective decision-making process, allowing leaders to tackle complex challenges with clarity and confidence.

The Bottom Line:

Balancing AI recommendations with human intuition is the key to optimal decision-making in complex situations. While AI offers powerful data-driven insights, human intuition provides the emotional intelligence, creativity, and context that AI cannot replicate. By combining the strengths of both, leaders can make more informed, empathetic, and innovative decisions that drive success. In the evolving landscape of leadership, mastering this balance will be essential for navigating uncertainty, managing complexity, and leading with confidence.

AI is revolutionizing leadership and decision-making by providing leaders with data-driven insights, enhancing their ability to navigate complex situations, and enabling faster, more accurate decisions. While AI excels at analyzing vast amounts of data, identifying patterns, and forecasting outcomes, human intuition adds the essential elements of emotional intelligence, creativity, and context. The most successful leaders are those who learn to balance AI's analytical power with their own judgment, making decisions that are not only data-driven but also empathetic, innovative, and well-rounded.

By leveraging AI as a tool for analysis and guidance, while trusting their instincts in situations that require emotional depth or creative thinking, leaders can optimize decision-making in a rapidly changing world. The synergy between AI and human intuition is the key to making smarter, more informed decisions that lead to better outcomes for organizations and individuals alike.

As AI continues to reshape leadership and decision-making, its influence extends beyond internal operations and strategic planning. In the next chapter, we will explore how AI is transforming networking and communication—essential skills for building relationships, collaborating, and expanding professional influence. From AI-powered platforms that enhance networking opportunities to tools that improve communication dynamics, AI is enabling individuals to connect and communicate more effectively than ever before. Let's dive into how AI is revolutionizing the way we interact, network, and communicate in both personal and professional settings.

CHAPTER 7: AI-POWERED NETWORKING AND COMMUNICATION

When Sarah first attended industry conferences as a marketing professional, she struggled to make meaningful connections. Amidst the sea of people, it was challenging to identify the right individuals to network with or know how to start impactful conversations. That all changed when she started using an AI-powered networking tool. The app analyzed her interests, professional goals, and social media activity to recommend potential connections who shared common goals or expertise. At her next conference, Sarah didn't waste time on surface-level conversations—she connected with industry leaders and potential collaborators who aligned with her professional objectives. With the help of AI, networking became not just easier, but more strategic and purposeful.

What if AI could help you build stronger, more meaningful relationships, both professionally and personally? In an increasingly digital world, AI is transforming how we connect, communicate, and cultivate relationships—helping us network smarter, communicate more effectively, and expand our influence.

According to a report by LinkedIn, **61% of professionals** say that regular networking is key to their career success, yet nearly **40%** struggle with the process. AI-powered tools are changing the game by facilitating connections and improving communication strategies, making networking more efficient and impactful for professionals across industries.

How AI Can Enhance Professional Networking and Relationship-Building

Networking has long been recognized as a critical factor in professional success. However, many individuals find it challenging to navigate the complexities of building and maintaining meaningful professional relationships. AI is changing the way we network by analyzing vast amounts of data, identifying potential connections, and even optimizing how we approach conversations. With AI-driven insights and recommendations, professionals can network more strategically, build stronger relationships, and unlock new opportunities for collaboration and growth.

1. AI-Powered Platforms for Intelligent Networking

AI-powered networking platforms are designed to help professionals connect with the right people, based on their goals, interests, and industry trends. These platforms leverage data from social media, career history, and even past interactions to suggest meaningful connections that align with a user's professional objectives. By identifying shared interests, complementary skills, and potential mutual benefits, AI eliminates the guesswork from networking, allowing individuals to focus on forming genuine connections.

- **LinkedIn and AI-Driven Connections:**
  LinkedIn, the world's largest professional networking site, uses AI to recommend connections based on your profile, job history, and interactions. Its AI algorithms analyze your network, the types of posts you engage with, and your industry to suggest potential contacts

who can help you achieve your professional goals. For example, if you're looking to expand into a new field, LinkedIn may recommend thought leaders or key figures in that industry, making it easier for you to engage in meaningful conversations that could lead to new opportunities.
- **Shapr for AI-Optimized Matchmaking:**
  Shapr is an AI-powered networking app that functions similarly to a dating app, but for professional relationships. Shapr's AI-driven algorithm analyzes your career interests, professional background, and networking goals to match you with other professionals who share similar objectives. This ensures that every connection you make is meaningful and relevant, helping you build a high-quality professional network that supports your career growth.

Key takeaway:
AI-powered platforms like LinkedIn and Shapr enhance networking by analyzing your professional goals and interests to suggest connections that align with your needs. These intelligent recommendations make it easier to build a network of valuable contacts who can support your career development.

2. AI for Personalized Relationship-Building

Networking is more than just collecting contacts; it's about building and nurturing lasting relationships. AI helps professionals foster these relationships by offering personalized insights into how to engage with contacts, track interactions, and stay connected over time. By leveraging AI's ability to analyze communication patterns and behavior, professionals can ensure that their outreach is timely, relevant, and valuable.

- **CRM Systems with AI-Driven Insights:**
  AI-powered customer relationship management (CRM) systems like **Salesforce Einstein** and **HubSpot** help professionals manage their contacts and maintain

relationships by tracking interactions and providing actionable insights. These systems analyze your communication history, social media interactions, and email exchanges to offer suggestions on when and how to follow up with contacts. For instance, if you haven't spoken to a potential business partner in several months, the CRM might suggest sending a personalized message or sharing an article of interest to keep the relationship warm.

- **Nudge.ai for Relationship Intelligence:**
Nudge.ai is another tool designed to improve professional relationship-building. It tracks your network's activity across social media and other platforms, providing you with insights into what your contacts are interested in, what they've been sharing, and how you can engage with them meaningfully. By offering real-time updates on your network's activity, Nudge.ai ensures that you can maintain relevant and consistent communication with key contacts, helping you nurture long-term professional relationships.

Key takeaway:
AI-driven tools like CRM systems and relationship intelligence platforms help professionals nurture their network by offering personalized insights into communication patterns and providing recommendations on how to engage effectively. This ensures that relationships remain meaningful and valuable over time.

3. Facilitating Collaboration and Expanding Opportunities

AI-powered networking tools don't just help you make connections—they also open doors to new collaboration opportunities by identifying synergies between you and your contacts. Whether it's finding potential business partners, collaborators for projects, or mentors who can guide your career development, AI makes it easier to identify and act on opportunities that can enhance your professional growth.

- **Ryze for AI-Driven Opportunity Discovery:**
  Ryze is an AI-powered platform designed to help professionals discover networking opportunities beyond traditional contacts. By analyzing your skills, professional history, and career goals, Ryze suggests opportunities for collaboration with others who have complementary expertise. Whether you're looking to co-author a paper, partner on a new project, or seek mentorship, Ryze uses AI to match you with individuals whose goals and abilities align with yours, creating high-potential partnerships.
- **AI for Mentorship Matching:**
  AI tools like **PushFar** are being used to match professionals with mentors based on their career goals, industry, and personal preferences. By analyzing the profiles and career paths of both mentors and mentees, AI can create highly personalized mentor-mentee pairings that foster meaningful learning and development. These AI-driven mentorship platforms ensure that professionals not only connect with the right people but also engage in relationships that are deeply aligned with their long-term objectives.

Key takeaway:
AI facilitates collaboration and expands opportunities by identifying synergies between you and your contacts. Whether through mentorship, partnerships, or collaborative projects, AI helps you discover valuable opportunities that might have otherwise gone unnoticed.

4. Building a More Diverse and Inclusive Network

One of the biggest challenges in traditional networking is the tendency to build networks that are limited to familiar circles or people with similar backgrounds. AI can help overcome this limitation by identifying and recommending connections that extend beyond your immediate network and include a more diverse range of people, skills, and perspectives. This leads to more inclusive networking practices, which can result in richer collaborations and broader opportunities for growth.

- **AI for Reducing Bias in Networking:**
  AI-powered networking tools like **Diverse Networker** are designed to help professionals build more diverse and inclusive networks. These tools analyze your existing network and provide recommendations to connect with individuals from different industries, backgrounds, and perspectives. By promoting diversity in networking, AI ensures that you're exposed to a wider range of ideas and opportunities, helping you grow both personally and professionally.

- **Expanding Horizons with AI:**
  AI networking tools can also help professionals overcome geographical barriers, enabling them to connect with individuals from across the globe. For instance, platforms like **Ten Thousand Coffees** use AI to match professionals from different regions, industries, and career stages, creating opportunities for international collaboration and cross-cultural networking. This global reach allows professionals to build a more diverse and dynamic network that enhances creativity, innovation, and problem-solving.

Key takeaway:
AI enhances diversity and inclusivity in networking by recommending connections that go beyond your immediate circles, introducing you to a wider range of perspectives and backgrounds. This leads to richer professional relationships and more innovative collaborations.

The Bottom Line:
AI is transforming professional networking by helping individuals connect more strategically, build meaningful relationships, and uncover new opportunities for collaboration. By leveraging AI-powered platforms, professionals can expand their networks, engage in personalized relationship-building,

and create a more diverse and inclusive professional community. As AI continues to evolve, it will play an even greater role in enhancing how we connect, collaborate, and grow in the modern workforce.

AI-Driven Tools for Improving Communication and Collaboration

In today's increasingly digital and remote work environment, effective communication and collaboration are more important than ever. However, maintaining clear, productive communication across teams, departments, or even entire organizations can be a challenge, especially when coordinating across different time zones, cultures, and platforms. AI-driven tools are stepping in to help bridge these gaps by streamlining communication, enhancing collaboration, and ensuring that interactions are more efficient, personalized, and productive. By leveraging AI, professionals can overcome common communication barriers and foster more cohesive, well-coordinated teams.

1. AI-Powered Communication Assistants

AI-driven communication assistants are becoming a central feature in helping professionals manage their day-to-day communications. These tools use natural language processing (NLP) and machine learning to assist with writing emails, messages, and documents more effectively, ensuring that communication is clear, concise, and tailored to the recipient. Whether it's crafting professional emails, responding to client queries, or generating reports, AI-powered communication assistants can save time, reduce errors, and improve the overall quality of communication.

- **Grammarly for AI-Assisted Writing:**
  Grammarly is an AI-powered tool that helps professionals improve the clarity and tone of their written communication. By analyzing grammar,

spelling, and sentence structure, Grammarly provides real-time suggestions that help users craft clearer, more professional messages. It also analyzes the tone of emails and documents, ensuring that your communication is appropriate for the intended audience—whether it's formal for business correspondence or more casual for internal team chats. This AI-driven feedback ensures that messages are clear and free from miscommunication, ultimately improving the quality of interactions.

- **Google Smart Compose for Email Efficiency:**
  Google's Smart Compose is an AI tool integrated into Gmail that suggests auto-completions for sentences as you type, helping to speed up email writing while ensuring clarity. By predicting common phrases and responses, Smart Compose allows users to craft professional emails more efficiently, reducing the time spent on drafting while maintaining a high standard of communication. Over time, the AI learns your personal writing style and can generate more personalized suggestions, making everyday email communication faster and more tailored.

Key takeaway:
AI-powered communication assistants like Grammarly and Smart Compose enhance the clarity, tone, and efficiency of written communication. These tools help professionals craft more effective messages, reduce errors, and save time, leading to improved communication across the board.

2. AI-Enhanced Collaboration Platforms

Collaboration platforms have become essential for teams working remotely or across different locations, and AI-driven features are now making these platforms even more powerful. AI enhances collaboration by improving how tasks are assigned, how teams interact, and how projects are managed. These tools enable teams to work together seamlessly, no matter where they are located, ensuring that communication is smooth and projects remain on track.

- **Microsoft Teams with AI-Powered Insights:**
  Microsoft Teams is a widely used collaboration platform that leverages AI to improve team communication and productivity. AI-powered features such as **real-time transcription** during meetings and **language translation** allow for smoother collaboration across teams that may be working in different languages. Additionally, Microsoft Teams uses AI to analyze meeting dynamics and provide insights into team interactions, helping leaders identify how to improve engagement and collaboration. For instance, it can track how often certain team members speak or provide feedback, giving leaders data-driven insights into team dynamics and suggesting ways to foster more inclusive discussions.
- **Slack with AI Workflow Automation:**
  Slack, another leading collaboration tool, uses AI to streamline communication and automate repetitive tasks. With **Slack's AI-driven workflow automation**, teams can create custom workflows that automatically assign tasks, send reminders, and update team members on project status. This helps reduce manual oversight and ensures that important tasks don't fall through the cracks. By automating routine tasks, Slack's AI allows teams to focus on more strategic and creative aspects of their work, improving overall productivity and collaboration.

Key takeaway:

AI-enhanced collaboration platforms like Microsoft Teams and Slack improve communication and project management by automating routine tasks, offering real-time insights, and facilitating cross-cultural collaboration. These tools help teams work more efficiently, even in remote or global settings.

3. AI for Real-Time Language Translation

In today's globalized world, professionals often work with colleagues, clients, and partners from different countries and cultures. Language barriers can present significant challenges in communication, leading to misunderstandings or delays in collaboration. AI-driven translation tools are helping bridge this gap by offering real-time translations of text and speech, making it easier for teams to communicate seamlessly across different languages.

- **Google Translate for AI-Powered Multilingual Communication:**
  Google Translate is one of the most well-known AI-powered translation tools that provides real-time translation of text and speech in over 100 languages. It's widely used in professional settings to facilitate communication between teams and clients who speak different languages. Whether in written documents, emails, or live conversations, Google Translate ensures that language differences don't become a barrier to effective communication. This AI-driven tool can also be integrated into collaboration platforms like Slack or Microsoft Teams, allowing for multilingual communication within project discussions.

- **Zoom's Real-Time Translation for Global Collaboration:**
  As remote work becomes more prevalent, platforms like **Zoom** are integrating AI-driven translation features to help teams collaborate in real-time across different languages. Zoom's AI-powered **real-time language translation** allows participants to speak in their native language while the AI translates the conversation for others, reducing misunderstandings and promoting smoother communication. This feature is particularly valuable for global teams that need to collaborate on complex projects without the

friction of language barriers.

Key takeaway:
AI-powered translation tools like Google Translate and Zoom's real-time translation feature enable seamless communication across languages, ensuring that language differences do not hinder collaboration. These tools make it easier for global teams to work together effectively, regardless of linguistic challenges.

4. AI for Improving Team Dynamics and Emotional Intelligence

Effective collaboration isn't just about managing tasks or communicating clearly—it's also about fostering a positive team culture and maintaining strong relationships between team members. AI is increasingly being used to analyze communication dynamics and provide feedback on how to improve team collaboration and emotional intelligence. By understanding team interactions and offering suggestions for improvement, AI helps leaders create more cohesive, emotionally intelligent teams.

- **Cogito for Enhancing Emotional Intelligence in Communication:**
  Cogito is an AI tool that analyzes voice patterns during conversations to detect emotional cues such as stress, frustration, or enthusiasm. By providing real-time feedback on emotional signals, Cogito helps professionals adjust their tone and approach to improve communication dynamics. This is especially useful in customer service and team collaboration, where emotional intelligence plays a critical role in building trust and maintaining positive relationships. For team leaders, Cogito offers insights into how their communication style impacts team members, enabling them to foster a more supportive and inclusive work environment.
- **AI for Analyzing Team Collaboration Patterns:**
  Platforms like **Humanyze** use AI to analyze

communication patterns across teams, providing insights into how teams collaborate, share information, and make decisions. By analyzing email exchanges, meeting behaviors, and communication networks, Humanyze can identify areas where team dynamics might need improvement—such as uneven participation in discussions or a lack of cross-team collaboration. These AI-driven insights allow leaders to make data-informed decisions on how to improve team dynamics, ensuring more balanced and productive collaboration.

Key takeaway:
AI tools like Cogito and Humanyze help improve communication dynamics and emotional intelligence within teams by providing insights into emotional signals and collaboration patterns. These tools help leaders create more cohesive, emotionally intelligent teams that work more effectively together.

The Bottom Line:
AI-driven tools are revolutionizing how teams communicate and collaborate, making it easier to manage tasks, foster relationships, and work across language barriers. From AI-powered communication assistants that enhance clarity and tone, to real-time translation tools that enable global collaboration, AI is streamlining communication and ensuring that teams can work together seamlessly. By leveraging these tools, professionals can improve their communication skills, enhance collaboration, and foster more effective teamwork in any environment.

Using AI to Find Mentors, Business Partners, and Like-Minded Professionals

One of the most valuable aspects of professional networking is connecting with people who can help guide, support, and collaborate with you. Whether you're looking for a mentor to help you grow, a business partner to launch your next big idea, or like-minded professionals to exchange knowledge and opportunities, AI is transforming how we find these key relationships. With the ability to analyze your goals, experiences, and preferences, AI-driven tools are helping professionals discover and connect with people who align with their personal and professional growth paths.

1. AI-Driven Mentorship Matching

Finding a mentor can be a game-changer in a professional career, but it can be difficult to connect with the right person. Traditionally, mentorship relationships were formed organically or through word of mouth, but now, AI can assist by identifying potential mentors who match your career goals, personality, and values. AI-driven platforms analyze your career trajectory, skills, and aspirations to suggest mentors who can provide valuable guidance and insights.

- **PushFar for AI-Powered Mentorship:**
  PushFar is an AI-powered mentorship platform that matches mentees with mentors based on their career goals, skills, and interests. The AI algorithm takes into account both personal and professional preferences, ensuring that the mentorship pairing is mutually beneficial. For example, if you are a marketing professional looking to expand your leadership skills, the AI might suggest a mentor who has experience in marketing management and can offer guidance on team-building, strategic decision-making, or navigating corporate structures. By providing personalized mentorship recommendations, AI removes the guesswork from finding the right mentor.
- **LinkedIn's Career Advice Feature:**
  LinkedIn has integrated AI into its **Career Advice** feature, which connects users with mentors within their network or industry. The AI analyzes your

profile, career interests, and professional history to recommend individuals who are well-positioned to offer mentorship. This can range from short-term advice on specific projects to long-term guidance on career development. By leveraging AI, LinkedIn helps professionals build meaningful mentorship relationships, enabling them to benefit from the expertise and experience of those who have walked similar career paths.

Key takeaway:
AI-powered mentorship platforms like PushFar and LinkedIn's Career Advice feature help professionals find mentors by analyzing career goals, skills, and interests to suggest meaningful, personalized connections. This makes the process of finding a mentor more strategic and effective, ensuring that both parties benefit from the relationship.

2. AI for Identifying Business Partners

In the entrepreneurial world, finding the right business partner is crucial for success. Whether you're launching a startup or looking to expand an existing business, the right partnership can drive innovation, open up new opportunities, and bring complementary skills to the table. AI tools can now help entrepreneurs identify potential business partners based on shared goals, complementary expertise, and mutual interests, streamlining the process of finding the perfect collaborator.

- **CoFoundersLab for AI-Based Partnership Matching:** CoFoundersLab is an AI-powered platform designed specifically for entrepreneurs seeking business partners. By analyzing user profiles, skill sets, and startup goals, the AI suggests potential co-founders who complement each other's strengths and can work well together. For instance, if you're a product developer looking for a business partner with experience in finance or marketing, CoFoundersLab's AI can identify candidates who possess those

complementary skills. This targeted approach not only saves time but also increases the likelihood of finding a compatible partner who shares your vision.
- **AngelList for AI-Driven Startup Collaboration:**
AngelList is another platform that uses AI to match entrepreneurs with business partners, investors, and collaborators. Its AI analyzes a range of factors, including company stage, industry focus, and long-term goals, to recommend potential partnerships that align with your business objectives. By connecting entrepreneurs with like-minded professionals and investors, AngelList helps startups find the resources they need to grow and succeed.

Key takeaway:
AI tools like CoFoundersLab and AngelList are making it easier for entrepreneurs to find business partners with complementary skills and shared goals. These platforms use AI to match users based on professional compatibility, enabling founders to build partnerships that enhance their chances of success.

3. **Connecting with Like-Minded Professionals for Collaboration and Networking**

Beyond mentorship and business partnerships, AI is playing a major role in helping professionals find like-minded individuals for knowledge exchange, project collaboration, or simply expanding their professional network. Whether through niche industry platforms or broader networking tools, AI helps individuals connect with professionals who share similar values, interests, and career paths, facilitating deeper and more meaningful relationships.
- **Shapr for Networking with Like-Minded Professionals:**
Shapr is an AI-powered networking app that helps professionals connect with others who share similar career interests, goals, and values. Often described as the "Tinder for networking," Shapr uses AI

to suggest connections based on your professional background, interests, and geographic location. By swiping through recommended profiles, users can connect with individuals who may offer collaboration opportunities, industry insights, or networking potential. This AI-driven approach to networking ensures that users meet professionals who align with their interests, leading to more fruitful and targeted connections.

- **Bumble Bizz for AI-Driven Professional Networking:** **Bumble Bizz** is another AI-powered platform that focuses on connecting like-minded professionals for networking and collaboration. The AI behind Bumble Bizz takes into account your industry, skills, and professional goals to recommend potential connections that could lead to business opportunities or creative partnerships. For professionals seeking new collaborators, business clients, or simply a larger network, Bumble Bizz offers a streamlined way to meet people who are a good match for their professional pursuits.

- **Meetup for Finding Collaborative Opportunities:** **Meetup** uses AI to suggest events, groups, and individuals based on your professional interests and career aspirations. By analyzing your past activity and stated preferences, Meetup's AI recommends local or virtual events where you can connect with like-minded professionals in your field. Whether you're looking to collaborate on a project, learn a new skill, or simply network with others in your industry, AI ensures that you find the most relevant opportunities to grow your professional network.

Key takeaway:

AI-driven platforms like Shapr, Bumble Bizz, and Meetup enhance networking by connecting professionals with like-minded individuals who share their goals, values, and interests.

These tools make it easier to form meaningful, targeted connections that lead to collaboration, knowledge exchange, and professional growth.

4. Fostering Long-Term Relationships Through AI

AI doesn't just help professionals find mentors, business partners, or collaborators—it also plays a role in maintaining and nurturing these relationships over time. Through personalized recommendations and communication insights, AI tools can help you stay in touch with key contacts, ensuring that relationships remain strong and beneficial as both parties progress in their careers.

- **Nudge.ai for Relationship Nurturing:**
  Nudge.ai helps professionals maintain and grow their relationships by tracking interactions and providing insights on when and how to reconnect. Whether it's following up after a networking event, checking in with a mentor, or re-engaging with a business partner, Nudge.ai ensures that you don't lose touch with key contacts. By analyzing communication patterns and offering personalized reminders, the platform helps you build long-term, mutually beneficial relationships that support your ongoing professional development.

Key takeaway:
AI tools like Nudge.ai help foster long-term professional relationships by providing insights into communication patterns and offering reminders to stay connected. This ensures that the relationships you build through AI-powered networking tools continue to grow and provide value over time.

The Bottom Line:
AI is transforming the way professionals find mentors, business partners, and like-minded collaborators by analyzing career goals, skills, and interests to suggest meaningful connections. Whether through AI-driven mentorship platforms, entrepreneurial matchmaking tools, or networking

apps that connect like-minded individuals, AI is making it easier to build relationships that support professional growth and success. As AI continues to evolve, it will play an even more significant role in helping professionals build strong, long-lasting networks that lead to fruitful collaborations and career advancement.

AI is revolutionizing the way professionals connect, communicate, and collaborate, making networking more strategic, communication more efficient, and relationship-building more meaningful. From AI-powered platforms that match professionals with mentors and business partners, to tools that enhance communication dynamics and streamline collaboration, AI is helping individuals and organizations unlock the full potential of their networks. By leveraging AI, professionals can build stronger, more diverse relationships, find the right people to support their growth, and maintain these connections in ways that were previously difficult or time-consuming.

As AI continues to evolve, it's clear that it is reshaping not only how we connect but also how we collaborate and create. In the next chapter, we'll explore how AI is pushing the boundaries of human creativity, offering new tools and techniques for artists, writers, musicians, and innovators alike. From generating creative ideas to co-creating alongside human collaborators, AI is changing the landscape of creativity in profound and exciting ways.

In Chapter 8, we'll dive into the world of **AI and creativity**—examining how AI is inspiring new forms of artistic expression, assisting in the creative process, and even taking on a creative role itself. Whether in art, music, design, or writing, AI is challenging our traditional notions of creativity and expanding the possibilities for what can be imagined and brought to life. Let's explore how AI is becoming an indispensable partner in the creative process and discover the ways in which human ingenuity and AI innovation are merging to redefine creativity.

CHAPTER 8: AI AND CREATIVITY

When Maria, a freelance graphic designer, hit a creative block on a project, she turned to AI for help. She had a tight deadline, and her usual sources of inspiration just weren't sparking the creativity she needed. So, she decided to experiment with an AI-powered design tool. Within minutes, the AI generated a series of design ideas based on the brief Maria had inputted. Some of the suggestions were outside her usual style, but they opened up new perspectives. Inspired by one of the AI-generated concepts, Maria created a final design that her client loved—and the creative process took half the time she had anticipated. Maria realized that AI wasn't replacing her creativity; it was enhancing it, offering a fresh way to jumpstart ideas and break through mental roadblocks.

What if AI could become your creative partner, helping you generate ideas, refine your work, and unlock new levels of imagination? In a world where creativity has always been considered uniquely human, AI is emerging as an unexpected collaborator, changing the way we think about art, design, music, and more.

According to a 2021 study by McKinsey, **71% of companies** now use AI in some form of creative work, from generating marketing content to developing product designs. AI is not just automating tasks—it's opening new doors for creative expression, helping artists, writers, and designers push the boundaries of what's possible.

How AI Is Revolutionizing the Creative Process in Writing, Art, Music, and Design

Artificial Intelligence is no longer just a tool for automating tasks or analyzing data; it has become an integral part of the creative process across various industries. AI is revolutionizing how writers, artists, musicians, and designers generate ideas, execute projects, and bring their visions to life. By offering new forms of inspiration, enhancing creative workflows, and even acting as a co-creator, AI is breaking down the barriers of traditional creativity and opening up exciting possibilities for human ingenuity.

1. AI in Writing: From Idea Generation to Storytelling

AI's impact on writing spans a wide spectrum, from helping authors overcome writer's block to generating entire pieces of content. Tools powered by AI can analyze vast amounts of text, generate ideas, and even help writers refine their language and tone, making the creative process faster and more efficient.

- **AI for Content Creation:**
  Platforms like **OpenAI's GPT models** (like the one you're interacting with now) and **Jasper AI** are helping writers generate content based on simple prompts. These tools can assist with everything from blog posts to short stories, providing suggestions for plot points, character development, and even writing style. Authors and marketers alike use AI to brainstorm ideas or create first drafts, which they can later refine and personalize. While AI doesn't replace the human touch in storytelling, it significantly speeds up the process of ideation and content generation.
- **AI for Editing and Refinement:**
  AI-driven writing assistants like **Grammarly** and **Hemingway Editor** analyze grammar, style, and readability, helping writers refine their drafts with

greater precision. These tools can offer feedback on sentence structure, tone, and clarity, ensuring that the final piece is polished and professional. In the case of longer works, AI tools can even detect inconsistencies in narrative structure or help writers maintain a consistent voice throughout.

Key takeaway:
AI tools are revolutionizing the writing process by generating ideas, assisting with drafts, and offering advanced editing suggestions. These tools free up time for writers to focus on creativity and storytelling, enhancing productivity without sacrificing quality.

2. AI in Art: Pushing the Boundaries of Visual Expression

AI is playing an increasingly prominent role in the world of visual art, allowing artists to explore new mediums, styles, and techniques that were previously unimaginable. From generating artwork to enhancing creative workflows, AI is transforming how artists conceptualize and execute their visions.

- **AI-Generated Art with GANs:**
  Generative Adversarial Networks (GANs) are a type of AI that has gained prominence in the art world. Tools like **Artbreeder** and **DeepArt** allow artists to create completely new pieces of art by blending existing styles, colors, and concepts. Artists can input different visual elements, and the AI generates new images that push the boundaries of traditional design. For instance, **Obvious**, a Paris-based art collective, famously used GANs to create "Portrait of Edmond de Belamy," an AI-generated painting that sold at auction for $432,500. These AI tools provide fresh inspiration and new ways to experiment with visual expression.

- **Assisting Artists in Workflow:**
  AI tools like **Runway ML** and **DALL·E** (from OpenAI) help artists rapidly prototype and develop their ideas by providing quick visual outputs based on simple

textual descriptions. This allows artists to iterate on concepts more efficiently, freeing them from time-consuming tasks like manual sketching or complex 3D modeling. Instead, AI can handle the initial creative exploration, giving artists more time to focus on refining their vision and adding personal touches.

Key takeaway:
AI is transforming the art world by generating new forms of visual expression and enhancing the creative process. Artists can use AI to explore new styles, rapidly prototype concepts, and push the limits of traditional artistic boundaries.

3. AI in Music: Composing, Producing, and Enhancing Sound

AI's influence in the music industry is growing, from composition to production, and even live performances. Musicians are using AI tools to generate melodies, harmonize arrangements, and experiment with new sounds that might otherwise remain unexplored.

- **AI for Music Composition:**
  AI platforms like **Amper Music** and **AIVA** (Artificial Intelligence Virtual Artist) allow musicians to compose original tracks by inputting a few parameters like genre, mood, or instruments. These tools can generate entire musical compositions or assist with specific sections, such as chord progressions or harmonies. While the AI generates the core elements of the composition, musicians can then refine, modify, and personalize the output to suit their artistic vision. AI allows for faster idea generation and helps musicians overcome creative blocks by offering fresh musical ideas.

- **AI in Sound Production:**
  AI is also revolutionizing music production. Tools like **LANDR** provide AI-driven mastering services, analyzing audio tracks and applying professional-grade mastering techniques to ensure high-quality

sound. Additionally, AI-powered plugins in digital audio workstations (DAWs) can assist in tasks such as auto-tuning vocals, enhancing soundscapes, and even suggesting edits based on the overall tone and structure of a song.

Key takeaway:
AI is reshaping the music industry by assisting with composition, production, and sound engineering. Musicians can now experiment with new styles, generate melodies, and produce high-quality tracks with the help of AI tools, all while maintaining control over the creative process.

4. AI in Design: From Concept to Execution

In the world of design, AI tools are enhancing creativity by automating repetitive tasks, generating ideas, and providing real-time feedback on design choices. Designers across industries are using AI to streamline workflows, create complex visuals, and experiment with new styles.

- **AI for Graphic and Web Design:**
  AI-powered design platforms like **Canva** and **Adobe Sensei** allow graphic designers to create high-quality visuals more efficiently. **Canva** uses AI to suggest design templates, color schemes, and layouts based on the user's input, while **Adobe Sensei** assists with more advanced design tasks, such as photo manipulation, video editing, and dynamic web design. These AI-driven tools help designers create professional-grade content faster and with greater flexibility.

- **AI for Personalized Design:**
  Tools like **The Grid** use AI to create fully responsive websites based on a few initial inputs from the user. The AI generates personalized designs that adapt to the user's preferences, ensuring that the end result is tailored to both the designer's vision and the user's needs. In fashion and product design, AI is helping designers prototype new ideas, test different materials,

and even predict future design trends by analyzing customer preferences and market data.

Key takeaway:

AI is streamlining the design process by automating time-consuming tasks, suggesting creative ideas, and helping designers personalize their work. From graphic design to web development, AI tools are transforming how designers approach their craft, allowing them to focus on the more creative and strategic aspects of their work.

The Bottom Line:

AI is revolutionizing the creative process across writing, art, music, and design by offering new tools and techniques that enhance ideation, execution, and refinement. Whether it's generating content, composing music, producing artwork, or designing websites, AI is empowering creators to break through creative blocks, explore new possibilities, and push the boundaries of traditional creative workflows. As AI continues to evolve, its role in the creative industries will only expand, offering even greater opportunities for human-AI collaboration in the pursuit of innovation and artistic expression.

Tools for Co-Creating with AI and Enhancing Your Creative Projects

AI is not just a tool for automating tasks; it is increasingly becoming a creative collaborator, working alongside artists, writers, musicians, and designers to co-create and enhance creative projects. AI-driven tools offer the ability to brainstorm ideas, refine concepts, and bring creative visions to life faster and more efficiently. These tools can act as a sounding board for creativity, sparking inspiration while allowing creators to push the boundaries of their work. By integrating AI into the creative process, professionals in various fields are finding new ways to collaborate with technology to achieve their artistic and professional goals.

1. Co-Creating Art with AI Tools

AI-powered art tools have emerged as powerful collaborators for visual artists, helping to spark new ideas, assist with technical execution, and explore creative boundaries. These tools don't replace human creativity but act as co-creators, enhancing an artist's ability to generate and refine their work.

- **Runway ML for Artistic Experimentation:**
    Runway ML is an AI platform designed for creators across mediums, allowing them to experiment with generative models to create new visual art. Artists can upload their own images or datasets, and the platform's AI models generate alternative visuals or interpretations based on that input. By blending human input with AI's pattern recognition and generative abilities, Runway ML acts as a co-creator, opening up possibilities for artistic exploration that might not have been considered before. Artists can adjust parameters, tweak designs, and use the AI's output as a foundation for further creative work.

- **Deep Dream Generator for Surreal Imagery:**
    Deep Dream Generator is another AI tool that lets artists co-create by enhancing their existing work with a dreamlike, surreal quality. Originally developed by Google, Deep Dream uses a neural network trained on millions of images to generate complex, layered visuals based on the input it receives. Artists can upload an image or concept, and the AI produces an entirely new interpretation. This AI-human collaboration creates opportunities for artists to see their work from new perspectives, blending their artistic vision with the AI's ability to detect and amplify patterns, textures, and shapes.

Key takeaway:
AI tools like Runway ML and Deep Dream Generator allow artists to collaborate with AI by generating unique visual content and

exploring creative possibilities. These tools push the boundaries of what's possible in digital and traditional art, enabling artists to experiment and expand their creative horizons.

2. AI as a Writing Partner

For writers, AI offers new ways to brainstorm ideas, structure narratives, and refine content. By working with AI, authors can overcome creative blocks, generate fresh perspectives, and even co-create entire sections of text. AI tools enhance the writing process by providing inspiration and refining drafts, enabling writers to produce content that is both creative and polished.

- **Sudowrite for Collaborative Storytelling:**
  Sudowrite is an AI-powered writing assistant designed for fiction writers. It uses advanced language models to help authors brainstorm ideas, overcome writer's block, and refine their stories. Authors can input their work-in-progress, and the AI provides suggestions for plot twists, character development, or dialogue. Sudowrite's "Expand" feature can generate entire scenes based on a brief prompt or continue a storyline with surprising and creative input, allowing authors to co-create with the AI as a partner in storytelling. Writers can then tweak the AI's output to fit their style and narrative voice, ensuring that the final product retains their unique perspective.
- **Grammarly for Editing and Refinement:**
  While tools like Sudowrite assist in the creative aspect of writing, platforms like **Grammarly** enhance the editorial process. Grammarly uses AI to detect grammatical errors, improve sentence structure, and suggest changes for clarity and readability. Although Grammarly doesn't create content, it collaborates with the writer to ensure that the final piece is polished and professional, acting as an AI-enhanced editor that ensures quality without sacrificing creative flow.

Key takeaway:

AI tools like Sudowrite and Grammarly offer writers the chance to co-create and refine their work by generating new ideas, expanding narratives, and improving the readability of their content. These tools empower writers to collaborate with AI, unlocking fresh perspectives while maintaining creative control.

3. AI for Music Composition and Production
AI is becoming an essential collaborator for musicians and producers, offering new ways to generate melodies, compose tracks, and enhance sound quality. AI tools can assist musicians in experimenting with different sounds, genres, and compositions, speeding up the creative process and enabling new musical exploration.

- **AIVA for AI-Driven Music Composition:**
  AIVA (Artificial Intelligence Virtual Artist) is an AI platform designed to help musicians compose music in various genres. Musicians can input basic information such as the desired mood, tempo, and instrumentation, and AIVA will generate original compositions that serve as a starting point. Whether for film scoring, video game soundtracks, or personal music projects, AIVA's AI-generated compositions allow musicians to co-create with technology. Musicians can build on the AI's output, making adjustments, adding layers, and fine-tuning the composition to match their artistic vision.
- **Amper Music for Music Production:**
  Amper Music is another AI-powered tool that allows musicians and content creators to generate custom music tracks by choosing specific styles, moods, and instrumentation. The AI composes music in real-time, which creators can then customize and enhance. Amper Music is particularly useful for content creators who need original music for videos, podcasts, or commercials but may not have extensive music

production experience. The platform acts as a co-creator, allowing users to experiment with different sounds and compositions while guiding the creative process.

Key takeaway:

AI-driven music platforms like AIVA and Amper Music enable musicians to co-create by generating original compositions and providing a foundation for musical experimentation. These tools accelerate the creative process, allowing musicians to explore new sounds and genres while maintaining their unique artistic input.

4. AI in Design: Collaborating with AI for Personalized and Efficient Design

AI-driven design tools are transforming how graphic designers, web developers, and product designers approach their projects. These tools allow designers to co-create with AI by automating time-consuming tasks, offering design suggestions, and providing personalized feedback based on user preferences. Designers can focus more on the creative aspects of their work while AI handles the more technical or repetitive elements.

- **Canva's AI-Driven Design Suggestions:**
  Canva, a popular graphic design platform, uses AI to suggest templates, layouts, and color schemes based on the user's input. This allows designers to quickly prototype visuals while ensuring they align with their brand's aesthetic or project goals. Canva's AI-powered suggestions act as a creative collaborator, providing options that the designer might not have considered. The designer can then customize these suggestions to create unique and polished final products, whether for social media, marketing materials, or personal projects.
- **The Grid for AI-Powered Web Design:**
  The Grid is an AI-driven web design platform that automates the process of building and designing

websites. Users input their content, images, and design preferences, and the AI takes over, creating a fully responsive website that adapts to user interactions. Designers can collaborate with the AI by adjusting elements and offering feedback, which the AI incorporates into the design process. This co-creation model streamlines web design, making it accessible for designers of all skill levels while still allowing for personalized and unique outputs.

Key takeaway:
AI tools like Canva and The Grid enhance the design process by offering automated suggestions, handling technical tasks, and enabling designers to focus on the creative aspects of their projects. These platforms facilitate co-creation, allowing designers to collaborate with AI to produce high-quality, personalized work efficiently.

The Bottom Line:
AI-powered tools are revolutionizing creative industries by acting as co-creators, helping artists, writers, musicians, and designers generate and refine their work. From generating music compositions and story ideas to offering design suggestions and producing unique artwork, AI is enhancing the creative process by offering new perspectives, speeding up workflows, and providing personalized feedback. As creators continue to collaborate with AI, they are able to push the boundaries of their artistic expression while maintaining control over their final output.

Inspiring Examples of AI-Driven Creativity in Personal and Professional Contexts

AI is no longer just a tool for data processing or automation—it has become a catalyst for creativity across industries and personal projects. From producing stunning artwork and composing original music to assisting in product design and even writing novels, AI is inspiring individuals and professionals to explore new creative avenues. Here are some remarkable examples of how AI-driven creativity is making an impact in both personal and professional contexts.

1. AI in Art: Pushing the Boundaries of Visual Expression
AI-generated art has captured the world's attention, challenging traditional notions of creativity and artistic ownership. Professional artists, hobbyists, and even major galleries are embracing AI to produce innovative visual art that blends human intention with machine learning. AI tools, such as Generative Adversarial Networks (GANs), enable artists to co-create visuals that are both unpredictable and uniquely captivating.

- **Obvious Collective's AI-Generated Portrait**:
  In 2018, the Paris-based art collective **Obvious** made headlines when their AI-generated artwork, "**Portrait of Edmond de Belamy**," sold at Christie's auction for $432,500. The painting was created using a GAN, where the AI analyzed thousands of historical portraits and generated its own interpretation. This sale marked a turning point in the art world, showing how AI could be seen as a co-creator in fine art and even challenge the traditional role of the artist.

- **Refik Anadol's Data-Driven Art Installations**:
  Media artist **Refik Anadol** uses AI to transform large datasets into immersive art installations. By using AI to interpret data such as weather patterns, city dynamics, or cultural archives, Anadol creates mind-bending visual experiences that challenge the viewer's perception of reality. His work showcases how AI can take seemingly mundane data and convert it into art that is abstract, dynamic, and deeply meaningful. In installations like "Melting Memories," Anadol uses brainwave data to visualize the act of remembering, turning AI-driven data interpretation

into an emotional and sensory experience.

Key takeaway:
AI is inspiring new forms of artistic expression by allowing creators to collaborate with machines and interpret vast datasets in ways that would be impossible without technology. From auction-worthy portraits to data-driven installations, AI is pushing the boundaries of what art can be.

2. AI in Music: Composing Original Tracks and Enhancing Production

The music industry is another field where AI is making waves, helping musicians compose original tracks, improve sound production, and even explore new musical styles. AI tools assist musicians in generating compositions, suggesting harmonies, and producing final mixes—all while keeping the artist's vision at the forefront. This collaboration between AI and musicians is expanding what's possible in music production and pushing boundaries in genres from classical to electronic music.

- **Taryn Southern's AI-Composed Album:**
  Taryn Southern, a singer and songwriter, made headlines when she released "**I AM AI**," the world's first album composed and produced entirely with AI. Using tools like **Amper Music**, Southern collaborated with AI to create melodies, harmonies, and arrangements for the album. By inputting her creative preferences, Southern allowed the AI to compose tracks that she could refine and personalize. Her work showcases how musicians can partner with AI to co-create music in ways that allow them to explore new styles and generate compositions more efficiently.

- **David Cope's Algorithmic Music:**
  Composer and music professor **David Cope** has been exploring the intersection of AI and music for decades. His program, **Experiments in Musical Intelligence (EMI)**, analyzes the works of classical composers and generates new pieces in their style. While some have

criticized Cope's work for blurring the lines between imitation and original creation, his compositions, often indistinguishable from human-written works, demonstrate the powerful role AI can play in pushing musical boundaries. Cope's work raises important questions about authorship and creativity while offering a glimpse into the future of AI-driven music composition.

Key takeaway:
AI is revolutionizing the music industry by helping musicians compose and produce original works, often faster and with greater creative freedom. From Taryn Southern's AI-composed album to David Cope's algorithmic compositions, AI is offering new possibilities for musical creation across all genres.

3. AI in Writing: From Fiction to Marketing Content

AI is also making significant contributions to the writing process, from assisting authors with novel-writing to helping businesses generate marketing content at scale. By providing suggestions, automating parts of the writing process, and offering new creative ideas, AI is helping writers explore storytelling in innovative ways while reducing the barriers to content creation.

- **The First AI-Written Novel: "1 the Road":**
  Author and developer **Ross Goodwin** used an AI system to co-create a novel titled **"1 the Road"** in 2018. Goodwin connected sensors—like a camera, GPS, and microphone—to an AI program that generated text based on the data it received as Goodwin traveled from New York to New Orleans. The AI captured environmental data and turned it into a stream-of-consciousness narrative that was both surreal and poetic. While not entirely a traditional novel, "1 the Road" challenges our understanding of authorship and opens the door to new forms of literary creation that blend human input with AI's interpretative abilities.

- **AI in Marketing: Automated Content Creation**:
Companies like **Jasper AI** and **Copy.ai** are using AI to generate marketing content, from blog posts and social media captions to email newsletters. These AI platforms analyze customer preferences, keyword trends, and brand voice to automatically create content that is tailored to specific marketing goals. For businesses, this means faster content production and the ability to scale creative marketing campaigns without sacrificing quality or originality. AI-generated marketing content is transforming how companies communicate with audiences, offering personalized, data-driven narratives at scale.

Key takeaway:
AI is reshaping the world of writing, whether through novel-length projects like "1 the Road" or in business contexts where AI-generated content allows for efficiency and personalization. Writers, marketers, and businesses alike are finding new ways to leverage AI in both creative and professional settings.

4. AI in Product Design and Innovation

AI is driving creativity and innovation in product design, helping designers create more personalized, efficient, and user-friendly products. From fashion and industrial design to user interface (UI) and user experience (UX) design, AI is offering new ways to enhance creativity, streamline processes, and bring innovative products to market.

- **Iris van Herpen's AI-Enhanced Fashion Designs**:
Iris van Herpen, a renowned Dutch fashion designer, uses AI to create intricate, otherworldly fashion pieces. By collaborating with AI, van Herpen designs garments that push the boundaries of traditional fashion, blending technology with craftsmanship. She uses algorithms to design complex structures, from delicate textures to avant-garde shapes, producing clothing that looks like wearable art. Her work is

a powerful example of how AI is being integrated into high-fashion design, offering new possibilities for material innovation and aesthetic exploration.
- **Nike's AI-Designed Shoes**:
  Nike has been using AI to design custom athletic shoes that cater to individual users' needs. The company's **AI-driven product design** analyzes data from athletes' movements to create shoes that optimize performance. For example, Nike's **Flyprint** technology uses AI to produce 3D-printed uppers that are tailored to specific athletes based on their biomechanics. This AI-assisted process allows Nike to deliver highly personalized products that improve both comfort and functionality, demonstrating the potential for AI to revolutionize product design in industries beyond fashion.

Key takeaway:

AI is inspiring innovation in product design by enabling creators to develop personalized, data-driven products that meet individual user needs. From Iris van Herpen's futuristic fashion designs to Nike's AI-optimized athletic shoes, AI is driving creativity in how products are conceived, designed, and manufactured.

The Bottom Line:

AI is driving a new era of creativity across art, music, writing, and design, offering inspiring examples of how technology can enhance human ingenuity. Whether co-creating artwork that sells at prestigious auctions, composing music with unprecedented speed, or helping authors write novels in new and experimental ways, AI is proving to be a powerful partner in the creative process. As we continue to explore the potential of AI-driven creativity, it's clear that the collaboration between humans and machines is unlocking new possibilities in both personal and professional contexts.

AI is reshaping the creative landscape, acting not just as a tool but as a collaborative partner that enhances human imagination across writing, art, music, and design. By offering new avenues for inspiration, automating repetitive tasks, and pushing creative boundaries, AI allows creators to explore uncharted territories and bring their visions to life more efficiently. From generating novel artistic works to helping musicians compose tracks and designers create personalized products, AI is proving to be a valuable collaborator, empowering artists and professionals to elevate their creativity to new heights.

As AI continues to evolve, the integration of human creativity and machine intelligence will only deepen, leading to even more groundbreaking innovations in the arts and beyond. However, AI's influence is not limited to the creative realm; it is also making significant strides in areas that directly impact our well-being. The next chapter explores how AI is revolutionizing health and wellness, improving mental and physical health, and enhancing personal well-being through cutting-edge technologies.

In Chapter 9, we'll dive into the transformative role AI is playing in health and wellness. From personalized fitness plans and mental health support to predictive diagnostics and AI-driven healthcare solutions, AI is becoming an essential tool in helping individuals lead healthier lives. Let's explore how AI is empowering people to take control of their health and wellness in ways that were once unimaginable, bridging the gap between technology and well-being for a healthier future.

CHAPTER 9: AI FOR HEALTH AND WELLNESS

Emily had always struggled to maintain a consistent fitness routine. Between work, family obligations, and everyday stress, her attempts at staying healthy often fell by the wayside. That all changed when she downloaded an AI-powered fitness app. The app analyzed her daily schedule, tracked her activity, and even monitored her sleep patterns to create a personalized fitness plan. It sent her reminders at the perfect times, suggested quick exercises she could do between meetings, and adjusted her workouts based on her progress. For the first time in years, Emily felt in control of her health, and the positive results followed quickly—better sleep, more energy, and improved physical fitness. What she once thought was impossible became achievable with AI's help.

What if AI could not only help you maintain your health but actively guide you to improve it? From personalized fitness routines to mental health support, AI is transforming how we manage our well-being. In a world where stress and unhealthy lifestyles are common, AI is offering solutions that help individuals take charge of their physical and mental health.

A report by Accenture predicts that by 2026, AI applications in healthcare could create **$150 billion in annual savings** for the U.S. alone, thanks to advancements in diagnostics, treatment, and wellness management. With AI's capabilities expanding, individuals and healthcare providers alike are benefiting from more personalized, effective, and accessible health solutions.

How AI Can Be Leveraged to Improve Physical and Mental Health

Artificial intelligence is making significant strides in the health and wellness industry, offering solutions that can greatly improve both physical and mental well-being. By harnessing data, personalizing health plans, and providing real-time insights, AI-driven tools are helping individuals manage their health more effectively than ever before. From fitness tracking and nutrition planning to mental health support and stress management, AI is empowering people to take a more proactive approach to their health.

1. Personalized Fitness and Nutrition Plans

One of the most impactful ways AI is being used in health is through personalized fitness and nutrition programs. By analyzing data from wearables, fitness trackers, and user input, AI can create tailored exercise routines and dietary plans that adapt to individual needs, goals, and progress. These AI systems continuously monitor performance, making real-time adjustments based on activity levels, recovery, and health metrics such as heart rate or sleep patterns.

- **AI-Driven Fitness Apps:**
  AI-powered apps like **Fitbod** and **Freeletics** use machine learning to create customized workout plans based on a user's fitness level, goals, and performance. These apps adjust workout routines as users progress, ensuring that they remain challenging without being overwhelming. By taking into account factors such as previous workouts, recovery times, and personal preferences, AI tailors exercise plans to the individual, making it easier for users to stay motivated and

achieve their goals.
- **AI for Nutrition and Meal Planning:**
Tools like **Nutrifix** and **Yummly** use AI to analyze users' dietary preferences, nutritional needs, and even allergies or restrictions to suggest personalized meal plans. These apps go beyond generic advice by factoring in health goals such as weight loss, muscle gain, or balanced nutrition. They also provide recipe suggestions and shopping lists, making it easier for individuals to maintain a healthy diet. AI's ability to analyze vast amounts of data allows it to optimize meal planning in ways that are highly personalized and sustainable.

Key takeaway:
AI-driven fitness and nutrition tools help users create personalized health plans that adapt in real-time, providing guidance that is specific to their goals and capabilities. This level of customization increases the likelihood of long-term success by aligning plans with individual lifestyles and preferences.

2. Mental Health Support Through AI

In addition to physical health, AI is playing an increasingly important role in mental health care. AI-powered platforms are being used to offer emotional support, monitor mental health conditions, and even provide therapeutic interventions. These AI-driven tools make mental health support more accessible and can help individuals manage conditions like anxiety, depression, and stress.

- **AI Chatbots for Mental Health:**
AI chatbots like **Wysa** and **Woebot** offer on-demand mental health support, providing users with a virtual companion that can engage in conversations about their feelings, stress levels, or emotional well-being. These AI-powered chatbots use natural language processing (NLP) to understand users' emotions and offer guidance, such as cognitive behavioral therapy

(CBT) techniques, mindfulness exercises, or stress-relieving suggestions. For individuals who may be hesitant to seek therapy or who need quick mental health support, these AI tools can offer an accessible first step.

- **AI for Monitoring and Early Detection of Mental Health Conditions:**
AI is also being used to monitor mental health and detect early signs of conditions such as depression or anxiety. Platforms like **Ginger** and **Mindstrong** analyze user data from smartphones, wearables, or online interactions to identify patterns that may indicate mental health struggles. For example, changes in sleep patterns, activity levels, or even the way someone types or interacts online can signal mental health issues. By catching these signals early, AI tools can prompt users to seek help or offer personalized interventions before problems escalate.

Key takeaway:
AI tools for mental health provide accessible support and early detection of mental health issues. By using AI-powered chatbots and monitoring platforms, individuals can access emotional support in real-time and gain insights into their mental well-being, helping them manage stress, anxiety, and depression more effectively.

3. AI for Stress Management and Sleep Improvement

Stress and sleep issues are common health concerns that can have a significant impact on both mental and physical well-being. AI is helping individuals manage stress and improve their sleep by offering personalized relaxation techniques, tracking sleep patterns, and providing actionable feedback to optimize rest and recovery.

- **AI-Powered Stress Management Apps:**
Apps like **Calm** and **Headspace** use AI to offer personalized mindfulness exercises and meditation

sessions designed to reduce stress. These platforms analyze user preferences and habits, tailoring content that fits into daily routines and addresses specific stress triggers. AI can suggest specific breathing exercises, mindfulness practices, or guided meditations based on an individual's current mood or stress level, making stress management more targeted and effective.

- **AI for Sleep Tracking and Improvement:**
  AI-powered tools like **Sleep Cycle** and **SleepScore** monitor users' sleep patterns, analyzing factors such as movement, heart rate, and sound during sleep. These apps provide detailed reports on sleep quality, suggesting adjustments in lifestyle, sleep environment, or bedtime routines to help improve rest. Some AI-driven wearables, like **Oura Ring**, even use machine learning to predict optimal bedtimes and recovery times based on daily activity, enabling users to make informed decisions about their sleep hygiene.

Key takeaway:
AI-driven stress management and sleep improvement tools offer personalized solutions to reduce stress and optimize sleep. By analyzing patterns and offering actionable feedback, these tools help individuals improve their overall well-being by addressing key areas that impact both physical and mental health.

4. Chronic Condition Management with AI

For individuals living with chronic conditions like diabetes, heart disease, or asthma, managing health can be a daily challenge. AI is making it easier to monitor and manage these conditions by offering real-time insights, predictive analytics, and personalized health interventions.

- **AI for Diabetes Management:**
  Platforms like **Livongo** use AI to help individuals manage diabetes by providing real-time insights into blood glucose levels, offering personalized

recommendations, and sending reminders for medication or lifestyle changes. The AI continuously learns from the user's data, adjusting recommendations to better manage blood sugar levels and improve health outcomes.

- **AI for Heart Health Monitoring:**
AI-driven wearables like the **Apple Watch** and **Fitbit** offer heart rate monitoring that can detect irregular heart rhythms, such as atrial fibrillation, which may indicate an increased risk of stroke. By continuously monitoring heart data, these wearables provide real-time alerts and suggest when users should seek medical attention. AI tools also help cardiologists make better treatment decisions by analyzing large sets of heart data, offering predictive insights into heart health trends.

Key takeaway:
AI is transforming chronic condition management by offering personalized, real-time monitoring and recommendations. For individuals managing conditions like diabetes or heart disease, AI-driven tools provide the insights needed to make better health decisions and improve quality of life.

The Bottom Line:
AI is playing an instrumental role in improving both physical and mental health. From personalized fitness plans and nutritional guidance to mental health support and chronic condition management, AI offers highly customized solutions that cater to individual needs. By providing real-time insights, recommendations, and emotional support, AI empowers individuals to take control of their well-being and live healthier lives. As AI continues to evolve, its potential to revolutionize health and wellness will only grow, offering even more sophisticated and accessible solutions for personal health management.

AI-Powered Fitness Apps, Health Monitoring, and Wellness Tracking

Artificial intelligence is playing a transformative role in how individuals manage their physical health, fitness, and overall well-being. Through the use of AI-powered fitness apps and health monitoring tools, individuals can access personalized fitness routines, track health metrics in real-time, and receive recommendations that adapt based on their lifestyle and goals. These technologies make health and wellness tracking more accessible, efficient, and personalized, allowing people to take proactive steps toward achieving their health goals.

1. AI-Powered Fitness Apps for Personalized Workouts

AI-powered fitness apps are revolutionizing the way people exercise by creating highly personalized workout plans that evolve based on real-time performance and goals. These apps analyze user data such as fitness level, past workouts, and specific goals (such as weight loss or muscle gain) to generate customized routines. As users progress, the AI adapts workouts to remain challenging and effective, making it easier to stay motivated and consistent.

- **Fitbod for Dynamic Strength Training:**
  Fitbod uses AI to create personalized strength training workouts based on a user's exercise history, available equipment, and fitness goals. The app tracks progress over time and adjusts the difficulty and structure of the workouts based on the user's performance. For example, if a user consistently improves their strength in certain exercises, the AI increases the weight or repetitions in future workouts. Fitbod's AI also helps prevent overtraining by balancing muscle groups and optimizing recovery time, making it an ideal app for those looking to build muscle in a safe and sustainable way.
- **Nike Training Club for Variety and Flexibility:**

Nike Training Club leverages AI to offer a diverse range of workouts, from yoga and strength training to high-intensity interval training (HIIT). The app tailors recommendations based on user preferences and fitness goals, ensuring that workouts align with the individual's available time, space, and energy levels. By analyzing user feedback after each session, Nike Training Club's AI improves its recommendations, providing users with a variety of exercises to prevent boredom and maintain engagement.

Key takeaway:
AI-powered fitness apps like Fitbod and Nike Training Club make personalized fitness accessible to anyone, providing tailored workouts that adapt as users progress. These apps help people stay motivated, prevent injuries, and achieve their fitness goals more effectively.

2. AI for Real-Time Health Monitoring

One of AI's greatest contributions to health and fitness is its ability to monitor health metrics in real time through wearable devices and mobile apps. By tracking heart rate, sleep patterns, activity levels, and even more complex biometric data, AI-driven health monitoring tools offer insights that help individuals optimize their wellness routines and detect potential health issues early.

- **Apple Watch for Continuous Health Tracking:**
  The **Apple Watch** is a popular wearable that leverages AI to monitor a range of health metrics, including heart rate, blood oxygen levels, and physical activity. Its AI algorithms analyze this data to provide users with personalized insights into their overall health, recommending when to rest, exercise, or seek medical advice. The Apple Watch can detect irregular heart rhythms, notify users of elevated heart rates, and even prompt users to take mindful breathing breaks when stress levels are high.

- **Oura Ring for Sleep and Activity Monitoring:**
  The **Oura Ring** is an AI-powered health tracker that focuses on sleep quality, recovery, and overall physical activity. It uses advanced sensors to monitor sleep stages, heart rate variability, and body temperature, providing users with daily insights into how well they are resting and recovering. The AI analyzes this data and offers personalized suggestions for improving sleep hygiene, activity levels, and stress management. By understanding how well users recover from daily activities, Oura helps optimize their physical and mental well-being.

Key takeaway:
AI-driven wearables like the Apple Watch and Oura Ring enable real-time health monitoring, offering insights into heart health, sleep patterns, and daily activity. These tools provide actionable data that empowers users to make informed decisions about their health and wellness routines.

3. AI for Wellness Tracking and Habit Formation

Wellness tracking encompasses more than just physical activity and sleep—it includes managing stress, tracking nutrition, and forming healthy habits. AI-powered apps are helping users monitor these aspects of their wellness journeys, providing tailored insights and recommendations that promote long-term behavior change.

- **Noom for Habit-Based Weight Loss:**
  Noom is an AI-driven wellness app designed to help users lose weight and build healthier habits through behavioral science. The app's AI analyzes user behavior, such as food intake, exercise, and stress levels, and offers personalized coaching to guide users toward healthier choices. By focusing on long-term habit formation rather than short-term dieting, Noom empowers users to adopt sustainable lifestyle changes that promote both physical and mental well-being.

- **MyFitnessPal for Nutrition Tracking:**
  MyFitnessPal uses AI to make nutrition tracking easier and more personalized. By scanning barcodes, logging meals, and analyzing eating habits, the app's AI generates insights into daily calorie intake, macronutrient distribution, and overall nutritional balance. MyFitnessPal's AI also helps users set personalized goals based on weight management, fitness goals, or dietary preferences. With real-time feedback on food choices, users can make healthier decisions and stay on track with their wellness goals.

Key takeaway:
AI-powered wellness tracking tools like Noom and MyFitnessPal provide users with actionable insights into their habits, from nutrition to stress management. By focusing on long-term wellness and habit formation, these apps help users create sustainable lifestyle changes that improve overall health.

The Bottom Line:
AI-powered fitness apps, health monitoring tools, and wellness tracking platforms are making it easier than ever to take control of personal health. By offering personalized recommendations, real-time insights, and behavior-focused guidance, these AI-driven technologies empower users to make informed decisions and achieve their fitness and wellness goals. Whether tracking sleep, monitoring heart health, or forming better eating habits, AI is enhancing every aspect of health management, paving the way for healthier and more balanced lifestyles.

AI for Preventive Health and Early Detection

One of the most impactful applications of AI in health and wellness is its role in preventive health care and early detection of potential health issues. Through continuous monitoring, pattern recognition, and predictive analytics, AI can identify early warning signs of illness, prompting users to take action before problems escalate. This proactive approach to health care can help prevent chronic conditions, detect early symptoms, and improve overall health outcomes. With the help of AI-powered tools, individuals can stay on top of their health in ways that were previously difficult or impossible.

1. AI for Early Detection of Chronic Conditions

AI-powered health tools are now capable of detecting early signs of chronic conditions such as heart disease, diabetes, and hypertension by analyzing real-time data from wearables and health apps. These tools continuously monitor vital signs and health trends, flagging abnormalities that might indicate an underlying health issue. By catching these signs early, users can seek medical attention sooner, improving the chances of successful intervention.

- **KardiaMobile for Heart Health Monitoring:**
  KardiaMobile is an AI-powered device that allows users to take electrocardiograms (ECGs) at home, which are then analyzed by AI algorithms to detect irregular heart rhythms like atrial fibrillation (AFib). AFib is a common cause of strokes, and early detection can significantly reduce the risk. KardiaMobile alerts users if their ECG shows signs of AFib, prompting them to consult a doctor before a potential health crisis occurs.

- **Livongo for Diabetes Management:**
  For individuals managing diabetes, AI-driven platforms like **Livongo** offer continuous blood glucose monitoring and personalized coaching. Livongo's AI analyzes blood glucose levels in real-time and provides tailored recommendations based on the user's data. For example, the AI might suggest dietary adjustments, medication changes, or exercise recommendations to help users maintain healthy blood sugar levels. The platform also alerts users to patterns that may indicate their condition is

worsening, enabling them to address issues before they become serious.

Key takeaway:
AI-powered health tools like KardiaMobile and Livongo enable early detection of chronic conditions by continuously monitoring health data and providing actionable feedback. This proactive approach helps users manage their health more effectively and avoid serious complications.

2. Predictive Health Analytics for Personalized Care

AI's predictive capabilities are also transforming preventive care by analyzing user data and predicting potential health risks based on lifestyle, family history, and health patterns. By using these predictions, users and healthcare providers can take preventive measures to mitigate risks and ensure better long-term health outcomes.

- **Google's AI for Early Cancer Detection:**
  Google's AI research has shown promising results in using machine learning to detect early signs of cancer. For instance, Google Health has developed AI systems capable of identifying early-stage lung cancer and breast cancer by analyzing imaging scans with greater accuracy than human radiologists in some cases. This predictive AI technology can detect tumors or abnormalities in medical images that may go unnoticed during routine screenings, allowing for earlier diagnosis and treatment.

- **Zebra Medical Vision for Predictive Health Insights:**
  Zebra Medical Vision is an AI-driven platform that scans medical images like X-rays, MRIs, and CT scans to detect a variety of health conditions, including cardiovascular disease, osteoporosis, and liver disease. The AI analyzes these images and provides predictions on the likelihood of developing these conditions, helping doctors make more informed decisions about preventive care. This predictive capability allows

healthcare professionals to identify patients at higher risk for certain diseases and intervene early to prevent more severe health outcomes.

Key takeaway:
AI's predictive analytics are enhancing preventive care by identifying individuals at risk for serious health conditions before symptoms appear. By providing early warnings and tailored insights, AI helps both users and healthcare providers take preemptive action to maintain better long-term health.

3. AI for Early Mental Health Detection

Mental health issues often go undetected until they become serious enough to impact daily life. AI is now being used to analyze behavioral patterns, speech, and even social media activity to detect early signs of mental health disorders such as depression, anxiety, and stress. These early detections can prompt individuals to seek help before their mental health declines further, allowing for timely intervention and support.

- **Mindstrong for Cognitive and Behavioral Health Monitoring:**
  Mindstrong uses AI to monitor cognitive and behavioral health through smartphone usage patterns. The platform's AI analyzes how users interact with their phones—such as typing speed, word choice, and response time—to detect changes in mental health that may indicate depression or anxiety. By tracking these subtle changes over time, Mindstrong's AI can predict when a user might be experiencing mental health difficulties and offer personalized recommendations or connect them to a healthcare provider for further evaluation.

- **Ginger for Real-Time Mental Health Support:**
  Ginger is an AI-powered mental health platform that provides real-time emotional and mental health support. Through chat-based interactions, the AI monitors users' mood and stress levels, identifying

when they may be at risk of developing mental health issues. By offering proactive guidance—such as meditation exercises, coping strategies, or connecting users with a human therapist—Ginger helps individuals manage their mental health before issues escalate. The platform's AI algorithms are continuously learning from user interactions, making the mental health recommendations more personalized and effective over time.

Key takeaway:
AI is helping individuals and healthcare providers detect early signs of mental health conditions by analyzing behavioral patterns and providing real-time support. Platforms like Mindstrong and Ginger offer personalized care that can prevent mental health issues from worsening, leading to better mental health outcomes overall.

4. AI for Personalized Preventive Care Plans
AI's ability to analyze large amounts of data allows for the creation of highly personalized preventive care plans that align with an individual's health risks, lifestyle, and goals. By considering factors such as family history, activity levels, and diet, AI-driven platforms can provide users with tailored plans that focus on maintaining their health and preventing illness.

- **Ada for Symptom Checking and Preventive Care:**
  Ada is an AI-powered health app that uses a comprehensive symptom checker to assess users' health conditions. The app asks a series of questions about symptoms, medical history, and lifestyle, and then provides a possible diagnosis along with advice on preventive measures. Ada's AI helps users identify potential health issues early and offers personalized suggestions for preventive care, such as lifestyle changes, dietary adjustments, or medical check-ups, to keep users on a healthy path.

- **Pact for Preventive Health Insurance Plans:**
  Pact uses AI to create personalized preventive health

plans for individuals based on their health data and risk factors. The platform analyzes data from wearables, medical history, and lifestyle habits to recommend preventive measures such as regular screenings, vaccinations, and wellness activities. Pact partners with healthcare providers and insurers to incentivize users to follow their personalized care plans, making preventive health care more accessible and affordable.

Key takeaway:
AI-driven tools like Ada and Pact offer personalized preventive care plans by analyzing users' health data and providing actionable insights. These platforms help individuals take control of their health by offering tailored recommendations that promote wellness and prevent illness.

The Bottom Line:
AI is transforming preventive health care by providing tools for early detection of chronic conditions, mental health monitoring, and personalized care plans. By continuously analyzing health data and predicting potential risks, AI enables individuals and healthcare providers to take a proactive approach to health management. This not only improves health outcomes but also empowers individuals to take control of their well-being, making preventive care more accessible and effective than ever before.

AI is revolutionizing health and wellness by offering personalized care, improving early detection of conditions, and empowering individuals to take control of their physical and mental well-being. From AI-powered fitness apps that provide customized workout plans to health monitoring devices that track vital signs in real-time, AI enables a more proactive and informed approach to personal health management. With its ability to detect early signs of chronic illnesses and mental health issues, AI is not only enhancing individual wellness but also transforming the healthcare industry by making preventive care more accessible, efficient, and personalized.

As AI continues to evolve, its role in health and wellness will likely expand, offering even greater insights and solutions for maintaining a healthy lifestyle. However, with this growing influence comes the need to address important ethical considerations. The use of AI in health raises questions about data privacy, consent, and the ethical use of AI-generated insights in medical decision-making. As we move into the next chapter, we'll explore the broader ethical implications of AI, examining how these concerns are shaping the future of artificial intelligence in health, wellness, and beyond.

In Chapter 10, we will shift our focus to the ethical considerations surrounding AI. As AI becomes more integrated into various aspects of life—from healthcare to finance, education, and beyond—questions about privacy, bias, accountability, and transparency are increasingly important. How can we ensure that AI systems are designed and used in ways that are ethical and fair? What measures need to be in place to protect individual rights and prevent misuse of AI technologies? Join us as we delve into these critical issues and explore how the future of AI can be shaped by ethical guidelines and responsible practices.

CHAPTER 10: ETHICAL CONSIDERATIONS OF AI

When Sarah applied for her dream job, she was excited to learn that the company used AI to screen applicants. She had heard that AI could be more objective than human recruiters, and she felt confident that her qualifications would make her a strong candidate. However, after submitting her application, Sarah was surprised to receive an almost immediate rejection. Upon further research, she discovered that the AI screening tool had likely flagged her resume due to a gap in her employment history, a period when she took time off to care for a family member. Frustrated, Sarah began to wonder if the AI system truly understood her experience—or if it had unfairly filtered her out based on a narrow set of criteria.

As AI becomes more involved in decision-making processes that affect people's lives, we must ask ourselves: how do we ensure that these systems are fair, transparent, and free of bias? While AI promises efficiency and objectivity, it also raises important ethical questions about accountability and justice. Can we trust AI to make decisions that align with our values, or is there a risk of reinforcing existing inequalities?

According to a 2020 report by MIT Technology Review, **67% of AI models** used in hiring processes are found to carry significant biases, often favoring certain demographics or unintentionally penalizing others. This statistic highlights a growing concern: while AI can improve efficiency, it can also perpetuate existing biases if not carefully monitored and regulated.

The Ethical Dilemmas Surrounding the Use of AI in Personal and Professional Life

As artificial intelligence becomes increasingly embedded in both personal and professional settings, it brings with it a range of ethical dilemmas. While AI offers remarkable benefits —efficiency, accuracy, and personalization—its widespread use raises critical questions about fairness, transparency, and accountability. Whether it's the use of AI in hiring, healthcare, law enforcement, or even daily personal tasks like social media and shopping, the ethical implications of AI systems are becoming impossible to ignore. How do we ensure that AI serves everyone equitably, without perpetuating existing biases or compromising individual rights?

1. Bias in AI Algorithms
One of the most pressing ethical concerns with AI is its potential to perpetuate or even amplify biases. AI systems learn from historical data, which can often reflect societal inequalities and prejudices. If the data fed into an AI system is biased, the system will likely produce biased outcomes. This is particularly concerning when AI is used in critical decision-making processes, such as hiring, loan approvals, and criminal sentencing.

- **Bias in Hiring Algorithms:**
  AI is often used by companies to streamline recruitment processes, helping HR departments sift through hundreds or thousands of job applications. However, AI hiring tools can introduce significant bias into these processes. For example, if an AI system is trained on resumes from historically male-dominated industries, it may unintentionally favor male

candidates over equally qualified female candidates. In 2018, Amazon had to scrap its AI recruitment tool after discovering that it consistently downgraded resumes that included the word "women," reflecting historical gender imbalances in its training data.
- **Bias in Criminal Justice Systems:**
  AI is also used in law enforcement and criminal justice to assess risk and make recommendations for sentencing or bail decisions. Tools like **COMPAS**, which are designed to predict the likelihood of a defendant committing future crimes, have been found to disproportionately label Black defendants as high-risk compared to white defendants. This happens because the AI is trained on historical crime data that reflects existing racial disparities in law enforcement and sentencing. The ethical dilemma here is clear: while AI systems can offer efficiency, they also risk reinforcing systemic inequalities if not carefully monitored and audited.

Key takeaway:
AI algorithms can introduce or perpetuate biases, particularly when trained on historical data that reflects societal prejudices. Ethical AI development must prioritize fairness by addressing these biases and ensuring that AI systems are not only efficient but also equitable.

2. Privacy Concerns and Data Security

Another significant ethical issue surrounding AI is privacy. AI systems require vast amounts of data to function effectively —whether it's personal health information for a fitness app, financial data for loan assessments, or behavioral data for social media algorithms. While this data enables AI to make more personalized and accurate predictions, it also raises concerns about how that data is collected, stored, and used.
- **AI in Social Media and Targeted Advertising:**
  Social media platforms like **Facebook** and **Instagram**

use AI to analyze users' browsing habits, interactions, and personal data to deliver highly targeted ads. While this can enhance user experience by providing relevant content, it also poses a significant privacy concern. Users may feel uncomfortable knowing that AI is tracking their every move online and making predictions about their preferences. Moreover, there have been instances where AI-driven data collection has been used for manipulative purposes, such as in the **Cambridge Analytica** scandal, where personal data was used to influence political campaigns without users' consent.

- **AI in Healthcare and Data Security:**
  AI's role in healthcare is growing, with systems being used to analyze patient data, diagnose illnesses, and recommend treatments. However, the use of sensitive health data raises ethical questions about data security and patient privacy. If AI systems are hacked or mishandled, individuals' private health information could be exposed or exploited. Furthermore, there are concerns about who owns the data—do patients maintain control over their personal health information, or does it become the property of healthcare providers or tech companies?

Key takeaway:
AI systems rely on vast amounts of personal data, which raises significant privacy and security concerns. It is crucial to establish clear guidelines for how data is collected, stored, and used, ensuring that individuals' privacy is protected and that AI systems are transparent about their data practices.

3. Accountability and Transparency

A major ethical dilemma with AI is the issue of accountability. When AI systems make decisions—whether it's approving a loan, diagnosing a patient, or deciding which job applicants to interview—who is responsible for those decisions? If an AI system produces a biased outcome, makes a mistake, or causes harm, who is held accountable: the AI developers, the company using the AI, or the AI itself?

- **The Black Box Problem:**
  One of the challenges with AI is its complexity. Many AI systems, particularly those that rely on deep learning, are often described as "black boxes" because even the engineers who build them may not fully understand how they arrive at certain decisions. This lack of transparency makes it difficult to hold anyone accountable when things go wrong. For example, if an AI system wrongly denies a loan application or makes a biased hiring decision, it can be challenging to pinpoint exactly where the problem occurred. This lack of transparency not only erodes trust in AI but also complicates efforts to ensure accountability.
- **Ethical AI Development and Regulation:**
  There is a growing push for stronger regulations to govern the development and use of AI. Some experts argue that AI should be designed with built-in accountability mechanisms, such as explainable AI (XAI), which aims to make AI decision-making processes more transparent. Governments and regulatory bodies are also starting to introduce guidelines and frameworks to ensure that AI systems are developed and used ethically. For example, the European Union's **GDPR** (General Data Protection Regulation) includes provisions that give individuals the right to know how automated decisions affecting them are made and to contest those decisions.

Key takeaway:
The lack of transparency in AI systems, particularly those based on deep learning, makes accountability a significant ethical concern. To address this, developers and regulators must prioritize transparency and build mechanisms to ensure that AI decisions are explainable, fair, and accountable.

4. AI and the Future of Work: Ethical Implications for Employment

AI is transforming the workplace, automating tasks, and changing the nature of work across industries. While AI has the potential to improve efficiency and productivity, it also raises ethical concerns about job displacement and economic inequality. As AI systems take on more complex roles, there is a growing fear that many jobs will be lost, particularly in industries like manufacturing, customer service, and transportation.

- **Job Displacement and Economic Inequality:**
  As AI and automation continue to replace human labor in certain sectors, there is concern that many workers will be left behind, particularly those in low-skill or repetitive jobs. While some argue that AI will create new opportunities in tech and other advanced fields, there is a risk that these opportunities may not be accessible to all workers, leading to greater economic inequality. For example, an AI system that automates warehouse tasks may improve efficiency for the company, but it could also displace thousands of workers who rely on those jobs for their livelihoods. The ethical question, then, is how to balance the benefits of AI-driven efficiency with the potential harm caused by job displacement.

- **AI for Workforce Training and Upskilling:**
  On the positive side, AI can also be used to help workers adapt to the changing job market by providing personalized training and upskilling opportunities. AI-powered learning platforms like **Coursera** and **Udacity** offer tailored courses designed to help individuals acquire new skills and transition into emerging industries. However, this approach requires investment and accessibility to ensure that all workers, regardless of background, can benefit from these

opportunities.

Key takeaway:
AI's impact on the future of work presents both opportunities and ethical challenges. While AI can improve productivity and create new jobs, it also risks displacing workers and exacerbating economic inequality. Ethical AI development should include strategies for mitigating these impacts, such as reskilling programs and support for displaced workers.

The Bottom Line:
The ethical dilemmas surrounding AI's use in personal and professional life are complex and multifaceted. From bias in algorithms and data privacy concerns to accountability and the future of work, AI presents both opportunities and risks that require careful consideration. As AI continues to play a larger role in our lives, it is essential that we address these ethical challenges through transparent, fair, and responsible AI development. Only by doing so can we ensure that AI serves the broader good, rather than reinforcing existing inequalities or compromising individual rights.

Ensuring AI-Driven Decisions Are Aligned with Personal and Societal Values

As artificial intelligence increasingly influences decision-making in various aspects of life—from healthcare and hiring to finance and law enforcement—it becomes essential to ensure that AI-driven decisions align with both personal and societal values. The challenge lies in building AI systems that are not only efficient and accurate but also ethical, fair, and respectful of the human values that shape our societies. When AI systems lack this alignment, the consequences can be profound: reinforcing inequalities, perpetuating bias, or making decisions that undermine human rights. To address these concerns, we must explore strategies for ensuring that AI systems are designed and used in ways that reflect the values we hold dear.

1. Value Alignment in AI Development

At the core of ensuring AI-driven decisions reflect societal values is the concept of **value alignment**. This means that AI systems should be designed to adhere to ethical principles and human values such as fairness, justice, and respect for privacy. However, aligning AI with values is not a simple task—especially when those values vary across different cultures, industries, and individuals.

- **Ethical AI Frameworks:**
  To help align AI systems with human values, various ethical frameworks have been developed. Organizations like the **European Commission** and **OpenAI** have proposed ethical guidelines for AI, emphasizing principles such as fairness, accountability, transparency, and privacy. These frameworks aim to ensure that AI development and deployment consider broader societal values rather than focusing solely on technical efficiency or profit. For example, the **European Union's AI Ethics Guidelines** stress the need for AI systems to be inclusive, non-discriminatory, and designed with the public good in mind.

- **Human-Centered AI Design:**
  Another approach to value alignment is to adopt a **human-centered AI** design philosophy. This means putting human needs, well-being, and values at the forefront of AI development. For instance, in healthcare, AI tools that assist with diagnosing illnesses or recommending treatments should prioritize patient autonomy and privacy, ensuring that patients retain control over their personal health data and decisions about their care. Human-centered AI focuses on creating systems that enhance, rather than replace, human judgment and compassion.

Key takeaway:

Value alignment is critical in AI development to ensure that AI systems reflect societal values and ethical principles. Frameworks like ethical AI guidelines and human-centered design approaches help developers prioritize fairness, transparency, and the public good.

2. Addressing Cultural and Individual Value Differences

While it's important to align AI with societal values, one of the challenges in doing so is recognizing that values can vary greatly across cultures, industries, and individual preferences. What is considered fair or just in one culture may differ in another, and even within the same society, individuals may prioritize different values based on their personal beliefs, experiences, and circumstances. Therefore, AI systems need to be adaptable and sensitive to these differences, ensuring they can operate ethically across various contexts.

- **Culturally Sensitive AI Systems:**
  One of the ways to ensure AI systems respect cultural diversity is by incorporating **cultural sensitivity** into their design. For example, an AI-powered customer service chatbot used in different regions of the world may need to adapt its responses based on local customs, languages, and communication styles. Similarly, AI systems used in law enforcement or social services should be mindful of cultural differences in behavior and community norms, ensuring that the decisions they support are fair and respectful to all groups. Companies like **Google** and **Microsoft** have developed guidelines for building AI systems that account for cultural differences, aiming to avoid one-size-fits-all solutions that could unintentionally cause harm or discrimination.

- **Personalization in AI for Reflecting Individual Values:**
  On an individual level, personalization is key to ensuring that AI aligns with personal values. AI

systems that are customizable can allow users to input their preferences, ethical concerns, and priorities. For instance, AI-powered recommendation systems, such as those used in media platforms like **Netflix** or **Spotify**, can be personalized to reflect users' tastes, but they could also be tailored to exclude content that conflicts with the user's values, such as avoiding violent or explicit material. In the healthcare industry, patients should have the ability to make personalized choices about their care, with AI systems adapting their recommendations to align with the patient's personal values and treatment goals.

Key takeaway:
AI systems must be adaptable to accommodate cultural and individual value differences. Culturally sensitive AI design and personalized AI solutions ensure that decisions made by AI respect and reflect the values of diverse groups and individuals.

3. Transparency and Explainability in AI Decision-Making

To ensure that AI-driven decisions align with societal values, it's essential that these decisions are transparent and explainable. One of the biggest concerns with AI systems—especially those that rely on complex machine learning algorithms—is the lack of transparency, often referred to as the "black box" problem. When AI systems make decisions that impact people's lives, it's important for those decisions to be understandable and justifiable. Without transparency, it's impossible to assess whether an AI's decisions align with the values of fairness, equity, or justice.

- **Explainable AI (XAI):**
  Explainable AI (XAI) is an area of research that focuses on making AI systems more transparent and interpretable. The goal is to ensure that AI systems can explain their decisions in a way that humans can understand, making it easier to identify when and how values are being respected or compromised.

For example, if an AI system denies someone a loan application, XAI would allow the applicant to understand the specific reasons behind the decision, whether it's based on credit history, income level, or another factor. This transparency not only builds trust in AI systems but also ensures accountability, as decision-makers can be held responsible for any unethical or biased outcomes.

- **Regulation and Auditing for Transparency:**
  In addition to technical solutions like XAI, regulation plays a key role in ensuring transparency in AI decision-making. Governments and regulatory bodies are increasingly calling for AI systems to be auditable, meaning that the processes and data used by AI to make decisions must be open to inspection. This can help prevent the misuse of AI, whether intentional or accidental, and ensure that the AI systems used in industries like finance, healthcare, and law enforcement are aligned with societal values. Regulations such as the **European Union's General Data Protection Regulation (GDPR)** already require companies to provide explanations for automated decisions that affect individuals, setting a standard for transparency and accountability.

Key takeaway:
Ensuring AI decision-making is transparent and explainable is crucial for aligning AI systems with societal values. Explainable AI (XAI) and regulatory oversight play important roles in making AI systems more accountable and trustworthy.

4. The Role of Ethical AI Leadership

Ensuring that AI-driven decisions align with personal and societal values requires strong ethical leadership within the organizations developing and deploying AI technologies. Ethical AI leadership involves not only creating AI systems that prioritize fairness, transparency, and inclusivity but also fostering a culture of ethical awareness and responsibility among developers, engineers, and decision-makers.

- **Ethics Committees and AI Governance:**
  Many organizations have begun establishing **AI ethics committees** to oversee the development and deployment of AI systems. These committees bring together experts from diverse fields—such as philosophy, law, and computer science—to review AI projects and ensure they adhere to ethical standards. By providing oversight and guidance, these committees help ensure that AI systems are designed to reflect societal values and mitigate potential harm. For example, tech companies like **Google** and **IBM** have established internal AI ethics boards that are tasked with reviewing the ethical implications of their AI projects and making recommendations for improvement.

- **Promoting a Culture of Ethical AI Development:**
  Beyond formal governance structures, it's essential for organizations to promote a culture of ethical AI development. This involves training developers and engineers on the ethical implications of their work and encouraging them to consider the societal impact of the AI systems they create. Ethical AI leadership means prioritizing long-term societal well-being over short-term profits and ensuring that AI development is guided by a clear ethical vision. Companies that take this approach can build greater trust with their users and the broader public while avoiding reputational damage caused by unethical AI practices.

Key takeaway:
Ethical AI leadership, including the establishment of AI ethics committees and fostering a culture of ethical awareness, is crucial for ensuring that AI-driven decisions align with societal values. Organizations that prioritize ethics in AI development can build more trustworthy, responsible AI systems.

The Bottom Line:
Ensuring that AI-driven decisions align with personal and societal values requires careful attention to value alignment, cultural sensitivity, transparency, and strong ethical leadership. By adopting ethical AI frameworks, developing explainable AI systems, and promoting ethical responsibility within organizations, we can create AI technologies that not only deliver efficiency and accuracy but also reflect the values we hold as individuals and societies. As AI continues to evolve, its ethical alignment will be key to building trust, fostering inclusivity, and ensuring that AI systems benefit everyone.

How to Leverage AI Responsibly for Growth Without Compromising Integrity

As artificial intelligence becomes an increasingly powerful tool for driving innovation and growth, it's essential to use AI responsibly to ensure that growth does not come at the expense of ethical integrity. Whether in business, healthcare, education, or personal development, leveraging AI responsibly means balancing the pursuit of efficiency and progress with a commitment to fairness, transparency, and the protection of individual rights. Responsible AI practices are not just about minimizing harm but also about using AI in ways that align with long-term societal and ethical goals, ensuring that both organizations and individuals can benefit from AI-driven growth without compromising their values.

1. Prioritizing Ethical AI Design and Development
One of the first steps in leveraging AI responsibly is ensuring that the design and development of AI systems prioritize ethical considerations from the start. This involves integrating ethical principles into the AI development process and ensuring that developers, engineers, and decision-makers are trained in the ethical implications of their work.

- **Ethics by Design:**
  Incorporating **ethics by design** means embedding ethical principles directly into the AI system's architecture. This approach ensures that AI systems are built with fairness, transparency, and accountability in mind. For example, developers should consider potential biases in their datasets and build safeguards to mitigate these biases, ensuring that the AI system doesn't produce discriminatory outcomes. Additionally, AI systems should be designed with transparency mechanisms so that their decision-making processes are explainable to users. By making ethics an integral part of the development process, organizations can ensure that their AI systems are aligned with societal values from the outset.
- **Developer Training and Ethical Awareness:**
  Training AI developers and engineers in ethical decision-making is crucial for ensuring responsible AI development. Ethical training can help developers recognize the potential risks and societal impacts of the AI systems they are creating, encouraging them to consider how their work might affect different communities. This training can also raise awareness about the importance of fairness, inclusivity, and privacy in AI systems, empowering developers to make informed decisions that prioritize integrity alongside innovation.

Key takeaway:
Ethical AI design and development should be a foundational part of any organization's AI strategy. By embedding ethics into the AI system's architecture and training developers on ethical principles, organizations can ensure that their AI-driven growth is both responsible and sustainable.

2. Ensuring Transparency and Accountability in AI-Driven Decisions

Another critical component of leveraging AI responsibly is ensuring transparency and accountability in AI-driven decisions. As AI becomes more integrated into decision-making processes—whether it's approving loans, diagnosing patients, or recommending products—it's essential that these decisions are explainable and accountable.

- **Explainability in AI Systems:**
  AI systems, especially those powered by machine learning, can be highly complex and difficult to understand. However, it's important that AI-driven decisions can be explained to both users and stakeholders. **Explainable AI (XAI)** ensures that AI systems are not "black boxes" but instead provide clear reasons for their decisions. For example, if an AI system denies someone a loan, it should be able to explain which factors influenced that decision, whether it's credit history, income level, or other variables. This transparency helps build trust in AI systems and ensures that individuals can contest or appeal decisions if necessary.
- **Auditing and Accountability Mechanisms:**
  Organizations must establish mechanisms for auditing and holding AI systems accountable. This involves regularly evaluating AI systems for potential biases, unfair outcomes, or harmful impacts. For example, in sectors like law enforcement or criminal justice, AI tools used for risk assessments or sentencing should be audited to ensure that they are not disproportionately impacting certain demographic groups. Similarly, in business, AI tools used for hiring or promotion decisions should be monitored for fairness and inclusivity. Accountability measures ensure that organizations remain responsible for the outcomes of their AI systems and take corrective actions if necessary.

Key takeaway:

Ensuring transparency and accountability in AI systems is critical for responsible AI use. Explainable AI and regular auditing practices help organizations maintain integrity by making AI-driven decisions understandable and ensuring that they are fair and justifiable.

3. Balancing Innovation with Ethical Boundaries

In the pursuit of growth, it can be tempting to push the boundaries of AI innovation without fully considering the ethical implications. However, it's essential to strike a balance between pursuing AI-driven innovation and respecting ethical boundaries that protect individual rights and societal values. Organizations must ask themselves not only what AI can do but also what AI should do.

- **Responsible Data Use and Privacy Protection:**
  AI's power lies in its ability to process vast amounts of data, but with that power comes the responsibility to protect individuals' privacy and autonomy. Organizations must ensure that the data they collect and use for AI systems is done so ethically and with the informed consent of the individuals involved. This includes complying with data protection regulations such as the **General Data Protection Regulation (GDPR)**, which requires organizations to be transparent about how they collect, store, and use personal data. Additionally, organizations should implement data minimization practices, ensuring that they only collect the data necessary for the AI system to function, rather than harvesting excessive amounts of personal information.

- **Setting Ethical Limits on AI Applications:**
  Not every potential application of AI is ethically acceptable. For instance, using AI for surveillance in ways that infringe on personal privacy or civil liberties, or developing AI systems for autonomous weapons, raises serious ethical concerns. Organizations must

establish clear ethical boundaries around how AI is deployed, ensuring that growth and innovation do not come at the cost of fundamental rights. By setting ethical limits on AI applications, organizations can prioritize responsible growth that aligns with societal values.

Key takeaway:

Balancing AI-driven innovation with ethical boundaries is key to leveraging AI responsibly. Organizations must ensure that data is used ethically, privacy is protected, and that AI applications respect societal values and individual rights.

4. Promoting Inclusivity and Fairness in AI-Driven Growth

As organizations leverage AI for growth, it's important to ensure that the benefits of AI are distributed fairly and inclusively. AI-driven growth should not disproportionately favor certain groups while leaving others behind. Promoting inclusivity in AI development and deployment is essential for ensuring that AI systems contribute to social good and create opportunities for all.

- **Inclusive AI Development and Deployment:**
  AI systems should be designed with inclusivity in mind, ensuring that they cater to diverse user groups and do not exclude or disadvantage certain communities. For example, AI systems used in healthcare should be trained on diverse datasets that reflect the experiences of different demographic groups, ensuring that the AI's recommendations are effective for all patients, not just specific populations. Similarly, AI tools used in education or finance should be designed to ensure that marginalized groups have equal access to the benefits of AI-driven growth. Inclusivity also involves actively involving diverse voices in the development process—ensuring that women, people of color, and other underrepresented groups have a say in how AI systems are designed and deployed.

- **Addressing Bias and Ensuring Fairness:**
  To promote fairness, organizations must actively address bias in AI systems. This involves using diverse and representative datasets, regularly testing AI systems for bias, and implementing corrective measures when necessary. For instance, if an AI system used in hiring decisions consistently favors certain demographic groups over others, organizations must adjust the system to ensure that it promotes fairness and equal opportunity. By addressing bias, organizations can leverage AI for growth in ways that contribute to a more equitable society.

Key takeaway:
Promoting inclusivity and fairness in AI-driven growth ensures that the benefits of AI are shared by all. By designing inclusive AI systems and addressing bias, organizations can ensure that AI contributes to social good and economic opportunity for diverse communities.

The Bottom Line:
Leveraging AI responsibly for growth requires a careful balance between innovation and ethical integrity. By prioritizing ethical design, ensuring transparency and accountability, protecting privacy, and promoting inclusivity, organizations can harness the power of AI to drive growth without compromising societal values. Responsible AI practices ensure that growth is sustainable, ethical, and aligned with the long-term well-being of individuals and society. As AI continues to shape the future, organizations that commit to responsible AI use will be better positioned to lead with integrity and foster trust.

As AI continues to play an increasingly central role in personal and professional life, the ethical considerations surrounding its use have never been more important. From addressing bias and ensuring fairness to protecting privacy and maintaining transparency, leveraging AI responsibly requires a deep commitment to ethical integrity. The choices we make today about how AI is developed and deployed will shape the future of technology and its impact on society. By embedding ethical principles into the design of AI systems, holding developers accountable, and promoting inclusivity, we can ensure that AI serves the broader good—driving innovation and growth without compromising fundamental human values.

However, the conversation around AI ethics does not end here. As we turn our attention to the next chapter, it's clear that AI is also making significant advancements in the financial sector. From managing personal finances to transforming investment strategies, AI is revolutionizing the way individuals and businesses approach financial growth. But how can AI be used effectively in finance, and what role does it play in shaping the future of wealth management? Let's explore how AI is powering financial growth and reshaping the investment landscape in Chapter 11.

In Chapter 11, we'll dive into the transformative role AI is playing in the world of finance. AI-driven financial tools are offering individuals and businesses new ways to optimize investments, manage risk, and pursue financial growth. From robo-advisors and automated trading algorithms to AI-powered wealth management platforms, AI is making financial decision-making more data-driven, efficient, and personalized. Join us as we explore how AI is reshaping the financial world and what it means for the future of investments and financial growth.

CHAPTER 11: AI IN FINANCIAL GROWTH AND INVESTMENTS

A few years ago, James found himself overwhelmed by the complexity of investing. Between his demanding job and family life, he struggled to stay on top of stock market trends and make informed investment decisions. That's when he turned to an AI-powered robo-advisor. The platform asked a few questions about his risk tolerance, financial goals, and timeline, and then it went to work. Within days, the AI created a tailored investment portfolio for him, balancing risk and reward according to his preferences. Over time, the AI continuously adjusted his portfolio, rebalancing based on market shifts and ensuring James stayed on track to reach his goals. For the first time, James felt confident that his investments were being actively managed without the need for constant attention—and his returns reflected that.

What if you could have your investments managed 24/7 by an AI that never sleeps, constantly optimizing your portfolio to maximize returns and minimize risks? AI-driven financial tools are doing just that, and they're not just for professional traders anymore—they're accessible to everyone.

By 2025, it's estimated that **90% of all stock trades** will be executed by AI algorithms and robo-advisors, according to a report by CNBC. With AI taking the reins in financial markets, individuals and businesses alike are turning to these systems to make faster, more data-driven decisions that were once only possible with a team of financial experts.

AI-Driven Tools for Personal Finance Management and Investment Strategies

The rapid development of artificial intelligence has transformed the way individuals manage their finances and make investment decisions. AI-driven tools are no longer reserved for large institutions or expert traders; they have become accessible to everyday individuals, offering personalized financial advice, portfolio management, and real-time market insights. These tools empower users to optimize their investments, manage risk, and achieve financial goals with unprecedented ease and accuracy. Here are some of the key AI-driven tools reshaping personal finance management and investment strategies today.

1. AI-Powered Robo-Advisors for Investment Management
Robo-advisors have gained immense popularity in recent years, offering a cost-effective, automated solution for managing investment portfolios. These AI-powered platforms use algorithms to analyze individual financial situations, risk tolerance, and goals, then create and manage a diversified portfolio tailored to each user. Robo-advisors continuously monitor and rebalance portfolios to ensure they remain aligned with the user's financial objectives.

- **Betterment and Wealthfront: AI-Driven Personal Investment Solutions**
  Betterment and **Wealthfront** are two of the most popular AI-powered robo-advisors, providing users with a simple, automated approach to investing. By answering a few questions about financial goals, time horizon, and risk tolerance, users can have a portfolio created for them, often consisting of low-cost index

funds or exchange-traded funds (ETFs). The AI systems continuously monitor the portfolios, automatically rebalancing them in response to market fluctuations and reinvesting dividends to maximize returns. These platforms also offer tax optimization strategies, using AI to minimize tax liabilities through techniques such as tax-loss harvesting.

- **AI for Personalized Risk Management:**
Robo-advisors offer more than just portfolio management; they help users understand and manage risk. AI-powered platforms use complex algorithms to assess a user's tolerance for risk, often asking questions about financial security, income, and future needs. Once the AI has a complete picture, it adjusts asset allocations to align with that risk tolerance. For example, a younger investor with a higher risk tolerance might receive a portfolio that skews toward stocks, while an older investor nearing retirement may be allocated more bonds for stability. This ability to tailor investments to personal needs is one of the reasons AI-driven robo-advisors are becoming a preferred option for many individual investors.

Key takeaway:
AI-powered robo-advisors like Betterment and Wealthfront provide personalized, automated investment management, offering users a low-cost and highly efficient way to grow their wealth. These tools make it easier for everyday individuals to invest in a diversified portfolio that aligns with their financial goals and risk tolerance.

2. AI for Real-Time Market Analysis and Insights

Another significant advancement in AI-driven personal finance management is the ability to access real-time market analysis and insights. In the past, this level of information was available primarily to professional traders or high-net-worth individuals who had access to financial analysts and research teams.

Today, AI has democratized access to real-time financial data, allowing everyday investors to make informed decisions based on the latest market trends, stock movements, and economic indicators.

- **AI-Powered Market Monitoring with Bloomberg GPT:** Bloomberg, a global leader in financial news and data, has incorporated AI into its data platform to help investors make sense of the vast amount of financial information available. **Bloomberg GPT** uses natural language processing and machine learning to analyze financial news, market trends, and company reports, generating real-time insights for investors. This AI-driven analysis helps users identify potential investment opportunities, monitor market movements, and stay informed about factors that could impact their portfolios.
- **AI for Predictive Analytics in Stock Trading:** AI is also being used to predict stock market trends and identify potential investment opportunities. **Kavout**, for example, is an AI-powered stock prediction platform that analyzes historical stock performance, market data, and news to generate "K Scores"—numerical rankings that help investors identify stocks with high potential. These predictive analytics tools use machine learning to detect patterns in the market that human traders might miss, offering a new level of insight for investors looking to make data-driven decisions.

Key takeaway:
AI-powered platforms like Bloomberg GPT and Kavout provide real-time market analysis and predictive insights, enabling individual investors to make informed decisions based on the latest financial data. This level of access and insight was once reserved for institutional investors but is now available to anyone with the right tools.

3. AI for Personal Finance Management

AI isn't just transforming investments; it's also changing how individuals manage their day-to-day finances. AI-powered personal finance apps help users track spending, budget more effectively, and make smarter financial decisions. These tools use data analysis to provide personalized insights and recommendations, helping users take control of their financial well-being.

- **AI-Powered Budgeting with Mint and YNAB:**
  Apps like **Mint** and **You Need a Budget (YNAB)** use AI to help users manage their personal finances. These apps track spending habits, categorize expenses, and provide personalized budgeting tips based on user behavior. For example, Mint's AI analyzes your spending patterns and provides alerts when you're overspending in certain categories or when bills are due, helping users avoid unnecessary fees. YNAB's AI-driven system encourages users to "give every dollar a job," helping them prioritize savings and manage their financial goals effectively.

- **AI for Financial Health with Cleo:**
  Cleo is an AI-powered financial assistant designed to help users improve their financial health. The chatbot-style app uses AI to analyze spending habits, offer personalized saving tips, and suggest ways to reduce debt. Users can interact with Cleo via text, asking for updates on their bank balances, setting savings goals, or getting advice on cutting unnecessary expenses. Cleo's AI-powered insights are tailored to each user's financial situation, helping them stay on track and make smarter financial decisions in real-time.

Key takeaway:
AI-powered personal finance apps like Mint, YNAB, and Cleo provide users with the tools they need to track spending, manage budgets, and achieve their financial goals. These platforms make it easier for individuals to stay on top of their

finances and improve their overall financial health.

4. AI-Driven Investment Communities and Social Trading

Another innovative application of AI in personal finance management is the rise of AI-driven investment communities and social trading platforms. These platforms combine AI insights with community-based investment strategies, allowing users to learn from others, share strategies, and make collective investment decisions.

- **eToro's Social Trading Platform:**
  eToro is a popular social trading platform that uses AI to help users follow and mimic the investment strategies of top-performing traders. The platform's AI analyzes the portfolios and performance of experienced traders, offering insights into their strategies and allowing users to automatically replicate their trades. This "copy trading" feature enables novice investors to benefit from the expertise of more experienced investors, while still retaining control over their own portfolios. eToro's AI also provides performance tracking, risk assessment, and personalized recommendations to help users optimize their investments.

- **Quantopian's AI-Driven Investment Community:**
  Quantopian is an investment community where users can create and share their own trading algorithms. The platform uses AI to evaluate and rank these algorithms based on performance, risk, and other factors. Investors can then use the highest-ranked algorithms to inform their own trading decisions. Quantopian democratizes access to advanced trading strategies, allowing individual investors to benefit from the collective intelligence of the community and AI-powered insights.

Key takeaway:
AI-driven investment communities and social trading platforms

like eToro and Quantopian provide a unique way for individuals to engage with the stock market, learn from top traders, and benefit from AI-analyzed investment strategies. These platforms foster a collaborative approach to investing, helping users grow their wealth with the support of AI and community insights.

The Bottom Line:
AI-driven tools for personal finance management and investment strategies are empowering individuals to take control of their financial future in ways that were once reserved for professional investors. From robo-advisors and AI-powered market analysis to personal finance apps and social trading platforms, AI is making financial management more accessible, personalized, and data-driven. By leveraging these tools, individuals can optimize their investments, manage risk, and make smarter financial decisions, ultimately leading to greater financial growth and success.

How AI Helps Predict Financial Trends and Optimize Portfolios

One of the most transformative aspects of AI in the financial world is its ability to analyze massive amounts of data, detect patterns, and make predictions about future market movements. By processing historical data, market trends, news events, and even social sentiment, AI-powered systems can offer valuable insights into future financial trends, helping investors optimize their portfolios. AI's predictive capabilities are not just faster than human analysis—they often reveal patterns and opportunities that might otherwise go unnoticed. This advantage allows both individual investors and institutional players to make more informed decisions, reduce risk, and maximize returns.

1. AI for Predicting Market Trends

AI systems excel at processing and analyzing large datasets in real-time, a task that would be impossible for a human analyst. By identifying correlations and anomalies across a variety of financial indicators—such as stock prices, economic data, interest rates, and geopolitical events—AI systems can generate highly accurate predictions about market trends. These predictions are invaluable for investors looking to time the market, capitalize on emerging opportunities, or hedge against potential downturns.

- **Sentiment Analysis and Market Predictions:**
  AI uses sentiment analysis, a process by which it scans and interprets the tone of news articles, social media posts, and even public statements, to predict how market sentiment might affect asset prices. For example, platforms like **MarketPsych AI** track investor sentiment by analyzing the language used in media reports and financial news. The AI can detect whether public sentiment about a particular company or industry is trending positive or negative, allowing investors to anticipate market shifts. A positive outlook on a stock, detected through sentiment analysis, might signal an opportunity for investors to buy in before the market catches up.

- **Pattern Recognition in Stock Movements:**
  AI-driven tools like **Kavout** or **Alpaca** employ machine learning algorithms to analyze historical stock price movements and identify patterns that signal future price action. By processing decades of data in a matter of seconds, AI can detect patterns of volatility or consistency that human traders might overlook. For instance, if a certain stock tends to rise after quarterly earnings reports but dip slightly before, AI can alert investors to these trends, helping them take advantage of cyclical patterns in the market.

Key takeaway:

AI's ability to predict market trends through sentiment analysis and pattern recognition provides investors with a significant advantage in identifying opportunities and avoiding potential risks. These predictions allow for more strategic investment decisions, giving investors the ability to react proactively rather than reactively.

2. AI for Portfolio Optimization

In addition to predicting market trends, AI plays a crucial role in helping investors optimize their portfolios. AI-powered portfolio management tools can analyze an investor's holdings, risk tolerance, and financial goals, then suggest adjustments to maximize returns while minimizing risk. These tools continuously monitor and rebalance portfolios based on real-time data, ensuring that they remain aligned with the investor's objectives as market conditions change.

- **AI for Dynamic Portfolio Rebalancing:**
  Portfolio rebalancing is essential for maintaining a desired level of risk and return. Traditionally, this process requires periodic reviews by human advisors, but AI systems have made this more efficient by automating it in real-time. AI tools like **Wealthfront** and **Betterment** use machine learning to continuously analyze portfolio performance and make small adjustments when necessary. For instance, if a particular asset class becomes too heavily weighted in a portfolio due to a sudden rise in value, the AI system can rebalance the portfolio by selling some of the over-weighted asset and reallocating the funds into other areas that are under-represented. This real-time, data-driven approach ensures that portfolios remain optimized for risk and return without the need for constant manual intervention.

- **Risk Management with AI Algorithms:**
  AI is also highly effective at optimizing portfolios by managing risk. AI-driven systems like **BlackRock's**

Aladdin platform use sophisticated risk management algorithms to analyze a portfolio's exposure to different risk factors—such as currency fluctuations, interest rate changes, or political instability—and suggest adjustments that help minimize potential losses. By analyzing a wide range of variables that might affect the portfolio's performance, AI ensures that investors are not overly exposed to any single risk factor, helping to preserve wealth in volatile market conditions.

Key takeaway:
AI-powered portfolio management tools help investors optimize their portfolios by automating dynamic rebalancing and managing risk. This continuous optimization allows investors to focus on long-term goals while minimizing the need for manual adjustments, ensuring their portfolios are consistently aligned with their financial objectives.

3. AI for Personalized Investment Strategies

One of the key strengths of AI in financial management is its ability to create personalized investment strategies that align with an individual's financial goals, risk tolerance, and time horizon. By analyzing a wide range of personal and financial data, AI-driven systems can craft bespoke investment strategies that are tailored to the specific needs and preferences of the investor. These strategies can be adjusted over time as the investor's goals or market conditions change.

- **Tailored Strategies with Robo-Advisors:**
  AI-powered robo-advisors such as **Ellevest** and **Wealthsimple** go beyond basic portfolio management by offering personalized investment strategies. These platforms take into account not only an investor's current financial situation but also future goals, such as saving for retirement, purchasing a home, or funding a child's education. The AI system considers factors such as income, savings rate, and target

retirement age to recommend an investment strategy that balances growth potential with the investor's time horizon. As market conditions evolve or personal circumstances change, the AI can adjust the strategy to keep the investor on track toward their goals.

- **AI for Tax Optimization:**
AI systems are also being used to optimize investment strategies for tax efficiency. For instance, robo-advisors like **Betterment** use AI to execute **tax-loss harvesting**, where they strategically sell losing investments to offset gains in other areas of the portfolio. The AI identifies opportunities to minimize the investor's tax liabilities, ensuring that the portfolio is not only optimized for growth but also for after-tax returns. This level of automation allows investors to benefit from tax-saving strategies that were once only accessible to high-net-worth individuals with dedicated financial advisors.

Key takeaway:
AI-driven platforms like robo-advisors offer personalized investment strategies that align with individual financial goals and risk tolerance. By optimizing for tax efficiency and tailoring strategies to an investor's unique situation, AI helps investors maximize returns and stay on track toward their financial objectives.

4. AI for Predictive Risk Management

In addition to identifying trends and optimizing portfolios, AI is playing a critical role in predictive risk management. By analyzing historical data and simulating potential future scenarios, AI systems can anticipate market volatility and help investors prepare for potential downturns. This proactive approach to risk management gives investors the ability to hedge their positions, reduce exposure to volatile markets, and protect their portfolios from sudden losses.

- **Scenario Analysis and Stress Testing with AI:**

AI-driven platforms like **Aladdin by BlackRock** use scenario analysis and stress testing to evaluate how a portfolio might perform under different market conditions. The AI simulates various macroeconomic events—such as recessions, interest rate hikes, or geopolitical instability—and assesses the potential impact on the portfolio. Based on these simulations, the AI can suggest strategies to mitigate risk, such as adjusting asset allocations or using hedging instruments to reduce exposure to vulnerable sectors. This predictive approach helps investors avoid significant losses and stay prepared for market fluctuations.

- **AI for Volatility Prediction:**
AI tools like **Kensho** are used to predict periods of heightened market volatility by analyzing patterns in historical data, market sentiment, and economic indicators. These predictions help investors make more informed decisions about when to enter or exit certain positions, as well as how to adjust their risk profiles during periods of uncertainty. By anticipating market swings, AI systems give investors a valuable advantage in managing risk and navigating volatile environments.

Key takeaway:
AI's ability to predict market volatility and manage risk proactively helps investors protect their portfolios and minimize potential losses. Through scenario analysis and volatility prediction, AI empowers investors to make informed decisions and optimize their strategies in uncertain market conditions.

The Bottom Line:
AI is revolutionizing how investors predict financial trends and optimize their portfolios. By leveraging powerful algorithms, machine learning, and real-time data analysis, AI helps investors

identify opportunities, manage risk, and create personalized strategies that align with their financial goals. Whether through predictive market analysis, dynamic portfolio rebalancing, or tax optimization, AI is empowering investors to achieve better outcomes with greater efficiency and precision. As AI continues to evolve, its role in financial growth and portfolio management will only become more integral, offering new opportunities for investors to succeed in an increasingly complex market.

Using AI to Achieve Financial Independence and Smart Wealth Management

Achieving financial independence is a goal many people strive for, and with the advancement of AI-driven tools, managing wealth and securing long-term financial freedom has become more accessible than ever. AI helps individuals not only grow their investments but also manage their finances more strategically, offering personalized insights, automated solutions, and intelligent wealth management strategies. Whether through smart budgeting, optimized investing, or long-term financial planning, AI is transforming how individuals plan for the future, empowering them to achieve financial independence more efficiently.

1. AI-Driven Budgeting for Financial Control

One of the first steps toward achieving financial independence is gaining control over your spending and saving habits. AI-powered personal finance apps and platforms are designed to help individuals track spending, create realistic budgets, and develop long-term financial plans. These tools use machine learning algorithms to analyze spending patterns, predict future expenses, and offer actionable insights to help users make smarter financial decisions.

- **AI-Powered Personal Finance Apps:**
  Apps like **YNAB (You Need a Budget)** and **Mint** use

AI to help users manage their day-to-day finances by tracking income, expenses, and savings goals. By analyzing historical spending patterns, these apps offer personalized budgeting advice, suggesting areas where users can cut back or allocate more funds to savings or investments. For example, YNAB's AI encourages users to adopt a proactive approach to budgeting by assigning every dollar a specific job, helping users build a buffer between paychecks and save for long-term goals like retirement or debt repayment.

- **Real-Time Spending Insights:**
AI-powered apps like **Cleo** provide users with real-time insights into their spending habits, identifying patterns and offering suggestions for improvement. For instance, if a user is consistently overspending on dining out, Cleo's AI can notify them of the trend and recommend a weekly budget for meals. By continuously monitoring financial behavior and providing timely feedback, AI helps users develop better money management habits, ultimately leading to improved savings and financial independence.

Key takeaway:
AI-driven budgeting apps like YNAB, Mint, and Cleo help users take control of their spending and savings, laying the foundation for long-term financial independence. By offering real-time insights and personalized budgeting advice, these tools enable individuals to make smarter financial decisions and build healthy financial habits.

2. Automated Savings and Investment Tools

AI has revolutionized savings and investment strategies by making it easier for individuals to save consistently and invest strategically, even without in-depth financial expertise. AI-powered platforms can automate savings processes, make personalized investment recommendations, and continuously adjust strategies to optimize returns—all without requiring constant manual intervention.

- **Automated Savings with AI:**
  Apps like **Digit** and **Qapital** use AI to help users save money automatically. These platforms analyze users' spending habits and financial behavior, then use machine learning to identify when and how much they can afford to save without disrupting their daily expenses. For example, Digit's AI continuously monitors cash flow and transfers small amounts of money into a savings account based on the user's historical spending and income patterns. By automating the savings process, these AI tools help users effortlessly build an emergency fund, save for future goals, or even allocate funds toward investments.

- **Micro-Investing with AI-Powered Platforms:**
  AI has made it easier for individuals to start investing, even with small amounts of money, through micro-investing platforms like **Acorns** and **Stash**. These apps round up everyday purchases to the nearest dollar and automatically invest the spare change into diversified portfolios. The AI system recommends portfolios based on the user's risk tolerance and financial goals, helping them gradually build wealth over time. By automating the investment process and making it accessible to everyone, these platforms provide an easy entry point for individuals looking to grow their wealth and achieve financial independence.

Key takeaway:
AI-powered savings and micro-investing tools like Digit, Qapital, Acorns, and Stash simplify the process of building wealth by automating savings and investments. These tools make it easier for individuals to start saving and investing consistently, helping them move closer to their financial independence goals.

3. AI for Long-Term Wealth Management and Retirement Planning

As individuals look toward long-term financial independence, AI can play a crucial role in managing wealth and planning for retirement. AI-driven wealth management platforms provide tailored financial advice, optimize portfolios for long-term growth, and help users plan for significant life events—such as retirement, buying a home, or funding a child's education.

- **AI-Powered Wealth Management Platforms:**
  Robo-advisors like **Betterment** and **Wealthfront** offer comprehensive wealth management services, making it easier for individuals to plan for their financial future. These platforms use AI to create personalized investment strategies based on each user's financial goals, risk tolerance, and time horizon. For example, Wealthfront's AI-driven planning tool can analyze how different life events—such as a career change, buying a home, or starting a family—might impact the user's long-term financial trajectory. By continuously adjusting investment portfolios to match life stages and financial goals, these platforms ensure that users remain on track for retirement or other long-term milestones.

- **Retirement Planning with AI:**
  AI is also making retirement planning more accessible and precise. Platforms like **Personal Capital** offer AI-driven retirement planning tools that analyze users' financial situations, project future income needs, and offer tailored advice on how much to save and invest. The platform's AI assesses factors such as inflation, market volatility, and changes in income to ensure users are adequately prepared for retirement. By providing a clear roadmap for reaching retirement goals, AI helps users make more informed decisions about how to manage their wealth over time.

Key takeaway:

AI-powered wealth management and retirement planning platforms like Betterment, Wealthfront, and Personal Capital help individuals optimize their long-term financial strategies. These tools provide personalized insights and continuously adjust portfolios, ensuring users stay on track to achieve financial independence and secure their future.

4. AI for Financial Health Monitoring and Goal Setting
Achieving financial independence is not just about saving and investing—it's also about maintaining overall financial health and setting realistic goals. AI-powered financial tools help users monitor their progress, stay disciplined, and make adjustments to their financial strategies as needed. Whether it's tracking debt repayment, adjusting savings rates, or identifying new investment opportunities, AI helps individuals stay focused on their long-term financial goals.

- **AI for Debt Management:**
  For individuals working toward financial independence, managing debt is a critical step. AI-powered platforms like **Tally** use machine learning to help users manage credit card debt more efficiently. Tally's AI evaluates users' debt profiles, interest rates, and payment history, then suggests a personalized repayment plan that minimizes interest payments and accelerates debt repayment. By automating payments and providing personalized advice, Tally helps users reduce their debt more effectively, freeing up resources for savings and investments.

- **Setting and Tracking Financial Goals with AI:**
  AI-driven platforms like **Personal Capital** and **YNAB** allow users to set specific financial goals—whether it's saving for a down payment, building an emergency fund, or reaching retirement—and track their progress over time. These tools offer personalized recommendations to help users adjust their savings rates, cut unnecessary expenses, or

increase investments based on changing financial circumstances. By continuously monitoring progress and offering actionable insights, AI keeps users accountable and motivated to achieve their financial goals.

Key takeaway:
AI-powered financial health monitoring tools like Tally, Personal Capital, and YNAB help users stay on track toward financial independence by managing debt, setting goals, and tracking progress. These tools provide personalized advice and accountability, ensuring that users can make adjustments as needed to stay focused on their long-term objectives.

The Bottom Line:
AI is playing a transformative role in helping individuals achieve financial independence and manage their wealth more intelligently. From AI-powered budgeting and automated savings to long-term wealth management and retirement planning, these tools empower users to take control of their financial futures. By providing personalized insights, automating essential processes, and optimizing investments, AI makes it easier for individuals to build wealth, stay disciplined, and reach their financial independence goals with confidence.

AI has transformed the landscape of personal finance and investments, providing tools that empower individuals to manage their wealth more effectively, make smarter investment decisions, and achieve financial independence. From AI-driven robo-advisors and personalized investment strategies to predictive analytics that optimize portfolios, the impact of AI on financial growth is profound. These technologies not only make wealth management more accessible to everyday investors but also provide them with the insights and automation once reserved for elite professionals. By leveraging AI responsibly, individuals can maximize returns, mitigate risk, and build a secure financial future.

As we move forward, it's clear that the influence of AI goes beyond just wealth management. In the next chapter, we'll explore how mastering AI can lead to lifelong success in every area of personal and professional life. Whether it's enhancing productivity, driving innovation, or fostering personal growth, AI offers tools and techniques that can help individuals thrive in an increasingly digital world. Let's discover how you can harness AI's power to achieve ongoing success, adapt to change, and stay ahead in today's fast-paced environment in **Chapter 12: Mastering AI for Lifelong Success**.

CHAPTER 12: MASTERING AI FOR LIFELONG SUCCESS

When Laura first heard about AI, she assumed it was something only tech experts or large companies could use effectively. However, when she incorporated an AI-powered task management tool into her daily routine, she was surprised by how quickly it transformed her productivity. Instead of feeling overwhelmed by her never-ending to-do list, the AI helped her prioritize tasks, block time for deep work, and even reminded her to take breaks. Within a few weeks, she noticed a significant boost in her efficiency and her stress levels dropped. What she had once thought of as a distant technology had become her personal productivity partner—helping her achieve more in less time.

What if AI could become your personal coach—helping you not only organize your life but also push you toward your most ambitious goals? The tools for lifelong success are already in your hands, waiting for you to unlock their full potential.

A study by Accenture found that companies and individuals who adopt AI-driven tools see a **40% increase in productivity** on average. This shows that mastering AI is not just about staying competitive—it's about unlocking a level of success that may have previously seemed out of reach.

The Future of AI and How to Stay Ahead in an AI-Driven World

The future of AI promises to reshape nearly every aspect of our lives—both personally and professionally. As AI continues to evolve, it will become increasingly intertwined with daily tasks, business operations, and decision-making processes. While this presents immense opportunities, it also introduces new challenges for those who want to remain competitive in an AI-driven world. The key to staying ahead lies in understanding the trajectory of AI, continuously learning how to leverage its capabilities, and adapting to the rapid technological shifts that are already underway.

1. AI's Growing Influence on Every Industry

AI's integration into industries like healthcare, education, finance, manufacturing, and entertainment is accelerating at an unprecedented pace. From enhancing operational efficiency to transforming customer experiences, AI is fundamentally changing how businesses function and deliver value.

- **AI in Healthcare:**
  AI is already revolutionizing healthcare by improving diagnostic accuracy, predicting patient outcomes, and personalizing treatment plans. For instance, AI-powered tools like **IBM's Watson Health** analyze vast amounts of medical data to assist doctors in diagnosing diseases and developing tailored treatment strategies. As AI continues to advance, it will play an even greater role in preventative medicine, drug discovery, and patient care.

- **AI in Education:**
  In education, AI is making personalized learning a reality. Platforms like **Coursera** and **Duolingo** use AI algorithms to adapt course content and pacing based on individual learning styles and progress. AI-powered tutoring systems provide students with real-time feedback and customized learning paths, ensuring a more effective and engaging learning experience.

- **AI in Finance:**
    AI's impact on finance is profound, with predictive analytics and automated decision-making transforming investment strategies, fraud detection, and risk management. AI-driven robo-advisors and algorithmic trading platforms are democratizing access to wealth management, while advanced AI systems like **Aladdin by BlackRock** help institutional investors optimize their portfolios and manage risk on a global scale.

Key takeaway:
AI's growing presence across industries underscores the need for individuals to stay informed and skilled in using AI tools relevant to their profession. Understanding the role AI plays in your industry and proactively seeking out opportunities to learn and apply AI skills will keep you ahead of the curve.

2. Staying Ahead in an AI-Driven World

The pace of AI innovation means that professionals in every field will need to continually adapt to new technologies to remain competitive. Staying ahead in an AI-driven world requires a combination of curiosity, continuous learning, and the ability to adapt to evolving tools and strategies.

- **Lifelong Learning with AI:**
    AI itself is a powerful tool for continuous learning. Platforms like **LinkedIn Learning**, **Udemy**, and **Khan Academy** use AI to recommend courses based on individual goals and learning progress, making it easier to stay up-to-date on the latest trends in technology and other fields. Professionals can use AI to customize their learning experiences, focusing on areas that are most relevant to their career goals. For example, if you're in finance, AI-powered learning platforms can recommend courses on algorithmic trading or data analysis, while a marketing professional might be guided toward AI-

driven customer insights and automation tools.
- **Embracing AI-Enhanced Workflows:**
  To stay ahead, individuals must also embrace AI-enhanced workflows that streamline tasks and boost productivity. Tools like **Zapier** and **Notion** use AI to automate repetitive tasks, freeing up time for more strategic work. Professionals who integrate these tools into their daily routines can improve efficiency, allowing them to focus on higher-level tasks that require human creativity and critical thinking. Staying ahead means not just using AI as a tool, but seeing it as a partner in achieving more impactful outcomes.
- **Developing AI Literacy:**
  As AI becomes more pervasive, developing AI literacy will become essential for professionals in every field. This doesn't mean becoming an AI engineer, but rather understanding the fundamentals of how AI works, its capabilities, and its limitations. Knowing how AI algorithms make decisions, how data influences those decisions, and how biases can be mitigated will help individuals navigate the ethical and practical challenges that AI presents. Many universities and online platforms now offer AI literacy courses designed for non-technical professionals, making it easier than ever to develop a foundational understanding of AI.

Key takeaway:
Staying ahead in an AI-driven world requires a proactive approach to learning and adaptation. By leveraging AI for continuous learning, integrating AI tools into daily workflows, and developing AI literacy, individuals can position themselves for success in a rapidly changing landscape.

3. Building Resilience in an AI-Driven Future

One of the most significant shifts that AI will bring is the need for greater adaptability and resilience. As AI automates more tasks and transforms industries, professionals will need to be flexible in their careers, open to new roles, and willing to continuously upgrade their skills.

- **Adapting to AI-Driven Job Shifts:**
  While AI will automate many repetitive tasks, it will also create new opportunities in areas that require human creativity, emotional intelligence, and complex decision-making. Professionals should focus on building skills that complement AI technologies—such as problem-solving, leadership, and strategic thinking—rather than competing with them. As new AI tools emerge, those who are able to adapt quickly and take advantage of these technologies will be the ones who thrive.

- **Leveraging AI to Enhance Human Skills:**
  Rather than seeing AI as a replacement for human work, the future of AI is about augmentation—enhancing human skills and capabilities. By using AI to handle routine tasks, individuals can focus on work that requires human judgment, empathy, and creativity. For instance, customer service professionals can use AI chatbots to handle basic inquiries, allowing them to dedicate more time to solving complex issues and building stronger customer relationships. In this way, AI will not replace human workers but empower them to perform higher-value tasks.

Key takeaway:
Building resilience in an AI-driven world means being adaptable, continually learning, and embracing the ways in which AI can enhance your skills rather than replace them. By focusing on skills that complement AI, individuals can remain competitive and create opportunities for success in the future.

The Bottom Line:
The future of AI is bright, but staying ahead in this AI-driven world requires an ongoing commitment to learning, adaptation,

and resilience. Understanding how AI will continue to shape industries and leveraging it to your advantage are critical to thriving in the years to come. As we continue through this chapter, we will explore how to master AI tools and strategies for lifelong success, ensuring that you remain competitive and ahead of the curve in an ever-evolving world.

The Skills You Need to Thrive in an AI-Driven Future

As artificial intelligence continues to permeate every aspect of life, staying competitive in an AI-driven world requires more than just technical knowledge. While understanding the basics of AI is important, the future will place an even greater emphasis on developing skills that complement and enhance AI's capabilities. These skills will allow individuals to work alongside AI tools, apply human judgment where needed, and adapt to the evolving demands of the workplace.

1. Creative Problem-Solving

AI excels at processing vast amounts of data, recognizing patterns, and providing solutions based on established parameters. However, it often lacks the ability to think creatively, particularly when faced with new or ambiguous situations. This is where human creativity shines. In an AI-driven world, those who can think outside the box, generate innovative solutions, and tackle problems that AI systems cannot easily resolve will be in high demand.

- **AI-Assisted Creativity:**
  While AI can assist in the creative process, such as by generating design ideas, composing music, or suggesting solutions, it still relies on human guidance to produce meaningful results. For instance, tools like **OpenAI's DALL·E** can create visual content based on textual input, but it's the human artist who decides which concepts to pursue and how to refine the output into something with emotional or cultural

significance. Developing the ability to combine AI's strengths with your creative vision will be a powerful asset in the future job market.
- **Innovation in Problem-Solving:**
In industries like healthcare, business, and engineering, complex problem-solving often requires innovative thinking that pushes beyond the data-driven suggestions of AI systems. Professionals who can integrate AI's capabilities with their own creative insights to devise novel approaches will have a significant advantage. For example, using AI to analyze vast sets of patient data may lead to medical breakthroughs, but it requires creative medical professionals to identify new research questions and design treatments that address patient needs in ways AI alone cannot.

Key takeaway:
Creative problem-solving is a uniquely human skill that will remain crucial as AI takes on more technical and analytical tasks. By combining AI's analytical power with human ingenuity, professionals can tackle complex challenges and drive innovation in their fields.

2. Emotional Intelligence and Leadership

While AI can automate tasks and optimize processes, it struggles with the nuanced understanding of human emotions, relationships, and social dynamics. Emotional intelligence (EQ) will be one of the most important skills in an AI-driven world, as leadership, empathy, and communication become even more valuable in an increasingly automated environment.
- **The Human Touch in AI-Driven Workplaces:**
As AI handles more administrative and technical tasks, human workers will focus on roles that require interpersonal skills. In customer service, for example, AI chatbots may resolve basic inquiries, but human representatives will still be needed to manage complex

interactions that require empathy, negotiation, or conflict resolution. Leaders who excel in emotional intelligence will also be better equipped to inspire and manage teams, particularly as AI changes the nature of collaboration and communication in the workplace.

- **Leading in a Hybrid AI-Human Workplace:**
  Effective leadership in an AI-driven world will require a new set of skills that focus on managing hybrid teams—where human employees work alongside AI systems. Leaders will need to understand how to delegate tasks to AI systems, manage the ethical considerations surrounding AI use, and foster a workplace culture that encourages creativity and critical thinking. Emotional intelligence will play a vital role in ensuring that teams remain motivated, engaged, and adaptable, despite the disruptions caused by AI integration.

Key takeaway:
Emotional intelligence and leadership skills will become even more critical as AI takes over routine tasks. Professionals who can lead with empathy, manage human-AI collaboration, and foster strong relationships will thrive in an AI-driven future.

3. Adaptability and Lifelong Learning

In a world where AI technologies are constantly evolving, the ability to learn and adapt will be essential for staying relevant. AI is accelerating the pace of change in nearly every industry, which means that workers will need to be flexible and open to continuous learning to keep up with new developments. Traditional education and training models will no longer be sufficient—success will depend on a commitment to lifelong learning.

- **Embracing a Growth Mindset:**
  One of the most important attitudes to cultivate in an AI-driven world is a **growth mindset**—the belief that skills and abilities can be developed through effort

and learning. With AI automating more routine tasks, professionals will need to shift their focus toward acquiring new skills that are relevant to their evolving roles. This may include learning how to use new AI tools, gaining expertise in data analysis, or developing creative and strategic thinking skills that AI cannot replicate. Those who embrace a growth mindset will be more resilient and better prepared for the changes ahead.

- **Leveraging AI for Learning and Skill Development:** Ironically, AI itself can be a powerful tool for lifelong learning. AI-powered learning platforms like **Coursera** and **LinkedIn Learning** provide personalized recommendations for courses, adapting to users' learning styles and progress. These platforms can suggest new skills to acquire based on industry trends, ensuring that individuals stay ahead of the curve. Moreover, AI can offer real-time feedback and interactive learning experiences, making the learning process more engaging and efficient. By using AI tools to enhance their own learning, professionals can stay adaptable and continuously upgrade their skillsets.

Key takeaway:
Adaptability and lifelong learning are crucial for thriving in an AI-driven world. Professionals who embrace a growth mindset and leverage AI-powered learning platforms will be better equipped to evolve alongside rapidly changing technologies.

4. Data Literacy and Critical Thinking

As AI systems become more prevalent in decision-making processes, understanding how to interpret and work with data will be a valuable skill. Data literacy—the ability to read, understand, and communicate data insights—will become increasingly important as AI-generated data drives more business, policy, and strategic decisions.

- **Understanding AI-Generated Insights:**

AI systems are often black boxes, producing insights or predictions without revealing the underlying processes that led to those conclusions. Professionals will need to develop critical thinking skills to evaluate the quality and relevance of AI-generated data. For example, a marketing manager using AI to analyze customer behavior should be able to question whether the data accurately reflects real-world trends or if there are biases in the algorithm that need to be addressed. By developing a strong foundation in data literacy, individuals can ensure that they use AI-generated insights effectively and responsibly.

- **Balancing Data with Human Judgment:**
While AI excels at analyzing data, there will always be a need for human judgment to interpret the results and make final decisions. Data can tell you what happened, but it often takes human intuition to understand **why** it happened and what to do next. For example, in financial markets, AI may predict stock price movements based on historical data, but human investors still need to consider external factors such as political instability or changes in consumer behavior that may not be captured by the AI model. The ability to balance AI-driven data with human judgment will be a key differentiator in an AI-driven world.

Key takeaway:
Data literacy and critical thinking are essential for making informed decisions in an AI-driven world. Professionals who can interpret AI-generated insights and apply human judgment to data will be better positioned to lead and innovate in their industries.

The Bottom Line:
As AI reshapes the future of work, the skills needed to thrive in an AI-driven world extend beyond technical expertise. Creative problem-solving, emotional intelligence, adaptability,

data literacy, and lifelong learning will be the cornerstones of success. By cultivating these skills and embracing AI as a tool for growth, professionals can stay competitive, remain agile, and continue to thrive in a rapidly changing landscape.

A Roadmap for Leveraging AI to Create Lasting Personal and Professional Growth

As AI continues to influence and reshape industries, the key to personal and professional success lies in understanding how to leverage AI for continuous growth. By strategically using AI tools, individuals can improve their productivity, enhance their decision-making, and unlock new opportunities for development. This roadmap provides actionable steps for integrating AI into your personal and professional life, ensuring that you not only keep pace with technological advancements but also use AI to build long-term success.

1. Identify Areas Where AI Can Enhance Your Life

The first step in leveraging AI for growth is identifying the specific areas where AI can provide the most value in your personal and professional life. AI's versatility means it can be applied to a wide range of tasks—from automating repetitive work to improving decision-making, learning, and creativity. Start by asking yourself where you feel overwhelmed, inefficient, or unable to achieve the results you want. These are prime opportunities to introduce AI tools.

- **Personal Productivity and Task Management:**
  If you often find yourself struggling to manage tasks, deadlines, and priorities, AI-powered productivity tools like **Trello** or **Notion** can help. These platforms use AI to organize tasks, prioritize work, and offer reminders based on deadlines or workload patterns. By automating scheduling and task management, you can free up mental space to focus on high-value activities

that drive growth.
- **Learning and Skill Development:**
  For personal growth, AI-powered platforms like **Coursera** or **Udemy** can suggest personalized learning paths that align with your career goals. By identifying gaps in your skillset and providing real-time feedback, these platforms help you focus on the areas that will have the most impact on your future success. AI can even help you track progress, ensuring that you stay on course with your learning objectives.

Key takeaway:
Start by identifying areas of inefficiency or growth potential, then explore AI tools that can support you in these areas. Whether it's enhancing productivity, improving learning, or streamlining daily tasks, AI can act as a powerful ally in achieving your goals.

2. Integrate AI Tools into Your Routine

Once you've identified key areas where AI can help, the next step is to integrate AI tools into your daily or weekly routine. The key to long-term growth is consistency, so it's important to build AI-powered systems that work seamlessly within your lifestyle and professional workflows.

- **Automate Repetitive Tasks:**
  Integrating AI into your workflow doesn't need to be overwhelming. Start by automating small, repetitive tasks that consume time and energy but don't require creativity or decision-making. Tools like **Zapier** can help you automate routine processes, such as sending follow-up emails, tracking expenses, or managing social media posts. As you gradually integrate more AI into your routine, you'll find that these small automations free up significant time for more meaningful work.
- **Use AI for Time Management and Goal Setting:**
  AI-powered tools like **RescueTime** or **Clockify** help

you track how you spend your time and optimize your daily schedule. These platforms use AI to analyze your productivity patterns, identify time-wasting activities, and recommend more efficient ways to allocate your time. By integrating these tools into your daily routine, you can set better goals, manage your workload more effectively, and ensure you're working on tasks that drive long-term growth.

Key takeaway:
Integrating AI into your routine starts with automating small, repetitive tasks and using AI-driven insights to optimize time management and goal setting. The more you incorporate AI into your day-to-day activities, the more time you'll have to focus on growth-driven work.

3. Leverage AI for Data-Driven Decision-Making

One of AI's greatest strengths is its ability to process vast amounts of data and provide actionable insights. By leveraging AI for data-driven decision-making, you can reduce the guesswork in both personal and professional decisions, ensuring that your choices are backed by real-time data and predictive analytics.

- **AI for Business Strategy:**
  In a professional context, AI can help you make more informed decisions about everything from market trends to customer preferences. Tools like **Tableau** and **Power BI** use AI-powered analytics to visualize data and uncover insights that can inform business strategy. Whether you're managing a small business or working in a corporate environment, AI-driven analytics tools can help you identify growth opportunities, anticipate market shifts, and refine your strategies to stay competitive.
- **AI for Financial Growth:**
  For personal finance, AI-powered investment tools like **Wealthfront** or **Betterment** use data analysis and

machine learning to optimize your portfolio, ensuring that your investments are aligned with your financial goals. AI can also help with budget management by analyzing your spending habits and recommending adjustments that align with your savings or investment objectives. By using AI for financial decision-making, you can achieve better outcomes with greater confidence.

Key takeaway:
AI's ability to analyze data and provide actionable insights can significantly improve your decision-making process. Whether you're using AI for business strategy or personal finance, data-driven decisions will help you grow faster and more effectively.

4. Embrace Continuous Learning with AI

In a world that is constantly evolving due to rapid technological advancements, continuous learning is essential for both personal and professional growth. AI not only helps you identify skills you need to develop but also accelerates the learning process through personalized recommendations and real-time feedback.

- **Create a Personalized Learning Plan with AI:**
  Platforms like **LinkedIn Learning** or **edX** use AI to tailor course recommendations based on your career goals, past learning experiences, and industry trends. These platforms allow you to build a personalized learning plan that addresses the most relevant skills for your growth. By focusing on the areas where you need the most improvement, you can accelerate your learning and apply new knowledge quickly to your career or personal projects.

- **Track Your Progress and Adapt:**
  AI-powered learning platforms also help you track your progress and adapt your learning strategy based on real-time feedback. For example, if you're learning a new programming language or a business strategy,

AI tools like **Duolingo** for language learning or **Udemy** for skill development will monitor your performance and adjust the difficulty or focus of lessons as needed. This ensures you're always learning at the right pace and focusing on areas that will drive the most improvement.

Key takeaway:
AI-driven learning tools provide personalized guidance and real-time feedback, making continuous learning more efficient and impactful. By embracing lifelong learning through AI, you can stay ahead of industry trends and ensure that your skills remain relevant in an evolving landscape.

5. Measure Success and Make Adjustments

Finally, lasting personal and professional growth requires ongoing evaluation of your progress and the ability to make adjustments as needed. AI tools can help you measure your success and ensure that your goals remain aligned with changing circumstances.

- **Set Measurable Goals with AI:**
  Using AI-powered tools like **Todoist** or **Asana**, you can set specific, measurable goals and track your progress over time. These tools allow you to break down larger objectives into manageable tasks, ensuring that you stay focused on achieving your long-term growth targets. AI can also help you identify when you're falling behind or need to adjust your strategy, offering insights into how you can stay on track.
- **Refine Your Growth Strategy Based on AI Insights:**
  AI tools can provide valuable insights into your productivity, learning, and decision-making processes. By regularly reviewing these insights, you can refine your growth strategy to ensure that you're making the most of your time and resources. For example, if an

AI tool identifies that you're spending too much time on low-priority tasks, you can adjust your schedule to focus more on high-impact activities that drive growth.

Key takeaway:
Use AI to set measurable goals, track progress, and refine your strategy over time. Continuous evaluation and adjustment, guided by AI-driven insights, will help ensure lasting personal and professional growth.

The Bottom Line:
Leveraging AI to create lasting personal and professional growth requires a clear roadmap. By identifying key areas for improvement, integrating AI tools into your routine, making data-driven decisions, embracing continuous learning, and regularly evaluating your progress, you can harness the power of AI to achieve your long-term goals. With the right strategy and AI support, you'll not only stay ahead in an evolving world but also unlock new opportunities for success and fulfillment.

Mastering AI is not just about staying ahead in a world increasingly shaped by technology—it's about unlocking your full potential for personal and professional growth. AI offers unprecedented opportunities to enhance productivity, make data-driven decisions, and continuously learn and adapt to a rapidly changing environment. By integrating AI tools into your daily life, embracing a mindset of lifelong learning, and cultivating the skills that complement AI's strengths, you can thrive in an AI-driven world. Whether it's improving your efficiency, advancing your career, or achieving financial independence, AI has the power to propel you toward your goals and help you achieve lasting success.

However, AI is not just a tool for the present. As it evolves, its potential to shape the future grows even greater. It is up to each of us to embrace this technology responsibly, use it to our advantage, and ensure that it serves us in a way that aligns with our values. By mastering AI, we can not only unlock our own potential but also help shape a future where technology enhances human progress.

As we wrap up our journey through **AI SuperPowers: Leveraging Artificial Intelligence for Personal and Professional Growth**, it's clear that AI is more than a technological trend—it's a transformative force that can empower us in every area of life. In the next and final section, we will bring together the key insights and strategies from this book, reflecting on how AI can be used not only to enhance individual growth but to foster a future of innovation, collaboration, and success for all. Let's look at how AI's impact on our lives will continue to evolve, and how we can continue to harness its power to shape a brighter future.

EPILOGUE

As we reach the end of this journey through the world of artificial intelligence, one thing is clear: AI is not just a tool for the future—it is an integral part of our present. It's already reshaping industries, enhancing productivity, and opening up new possibilities in ways we could have only dreamed of a few years ago. But as with any powerful tool, AI's true potential is only unlocked when we use it consciously, thoughtfully, and with a clear understanding of how it can serve us.

Throughout this book, we've explored the many ways AI can help us thrive—whether by improving decision-making, enhancing creativity, optimizing our finances, or propelling our careers forward. We've seen that AI is not something to fear, but rather a powerful ally that can elevate our capabilities, streamline our daily lives, and offer new paths for personal and professional growth.

But this is just the beginning. AI's impact is still unfolding, and the opportunities it brings will continue to evolve. The future will belong to those who are willing to embrace change, who are curious and adaptable, and who recognize that AI is not here to replace us, but to enhance what we are capable of achieving.

As you move forward, consider AI as part of your toolkit for success—one that can help you meet your goals, solve problems, and open new doors. Remember that mastering AI is not just about learning a new skill or adopting the latest technology; it's about adopting a mindset of growth, resilience, and innovation.

The world we are moving into is one where those who embrace AI will have a significant advantage. But it's not just about staying ahead in your career or making better decisions—it's about creating a future where technology empowers us to live more fulfilled, balanced, and meaningful lives. The true power of AI lies in its ability to help us unlock the best version of ourselves, making us more productive, creative, and insightful.

So, as you close this book and move forward, take with you the lessons and strategies you've learned. Whether it's using AI to streamline your daily tasks, improve your financial outlook, or continuously learn new skills, remember that the future is in your hands. AI is a tool, and you are the one who decides how to use it.

This is your moment to step into the future, to harness the superpowers that AI offers, and to shape a life that is more aligned with your goals, values, and aspirations. The world of AI is vast, and the opportunities it holds are limitless. All you have to do is seize them.

Katherine Gierszal

ACKNOWLEDGEMENT

I would like to acknowledge the assistance of ChatGPT, an AI language model by OpenAI, for helping me brainstorm ideas, organize content, and shape parts of this book. Its insights and suggestions were invaluable during the writing process.

I would like to acknowledge my amazing husband, Bob Gierszal. He supported me in every instance where I doubted myself and my ability to write this book. He encouraged me without fail, and gave me ice cream everytime I needed it. He is my knight in shining armor and my favorite human being.

ABOUT THE AUTHOR

Katherine Gierszal

Katherine Gierszal is a passionate advocate for personal and professional growth in an AI-driven world. With a diverse background in entrepreneurship, sales, homeschooling, and writing, Katherine brings a unique perspective to the intersection of technology and human potential. She has dedicated her career to helping others unlock their full capabilities by embracing new tools, technologies, and strategies for success.

Katherine's journey has been anything but conventional. As a mother of four and an experienced homeschooler, she honed her skills in adaptability, creativity, and leadership—qualities that have become the foundation of her approach to using AI for personal and professional growth. Over the years, she has launched successful ventures in gemstone jewelry, real estate, and online sales, always driven by a desire to inspire and empower others.

Katherine has also written extensively on personal development, persuasion, influence, authenticity and now the power of artificial intelligence, blending her knowledge of emerging technologies with practical advice for everyday life. Her passion for continuous learning and innovation is reflected in her work, as she strives to make complex concepts accessible to all.

In AI SuperPowers: Leveraging Artificial Intelligence for Personal and Professional Growth, Katherine shares her insights on how AI can be a transformative force for anyone looking to enhance their life, career, and future. Whether you're a seasoned professional or just beginning to explore the potential of AI, Katherine's guidance will empower you to use this technology as a tool for lasting success.

When Katherine isn't writing or exploring the latest in AI, she enjoys spending time with her family and pets, creating art, and discovering new ways to inspire others to reach their full potential.

BOOKS BY THIS AUTHOR

Master The Art Of Persuasion: Unlocking The Power Of Influence For Lasting Success

Master the Art of Persuasion and Influence: A Comprehensive Guide for Success in Life and Business
This book is an essential resource for anyone looking to unlock the secrets of persuasion and influence across all areas of life. With in-depth explorations of the science behind these concepts, the book offers practical strategies to develop and master authentic persuasion and influence.

Starting with Chapter 1, Understanding the Dynamics of Relationships, the book dives into how relationships play a pivotal role in influence and persuasion. Following this, Chapter 2 and Chapter 3 explore The Science of Persuasion and The Neuroscience of Persuasion, breaking down the mechanics of why and how people can be persuaded.

The book then examines The Science of Influence in Chapter 4, and the potential dark side in Chapter 5, The Science of Manipulation. From there, it highlights the power of authenticity in Chapter 6, The Science of Authenticity, helping readers understand how genuine connection fosters influence.

Further exploring key relationship dynamics, Chapters 7 through 9 focus on personal and family relationships as well as business relationships, emphasizing the role of authenticity in persuasion. Practical aspects like body language (Chapter 10) and charm (Chapter 11) are explored to help readers refine their influence skills.

Sales and networking also receive significant attention, with Chapters 12 through 14 covering The Perfect Sales Pitch, The Art of Sales Presentations, and Ninja Networking. The book doesn't stop at business—it takes readers through social media strategies (Chapter 15) and tips to gain attention from power players (Chapter 16).

The importance of influence in negotiations (Chapter 17) and ethical leadership (Chapter 18) are key topics, followed by crisis management and decision-making under pressure in Chapter 19, Building Influence in Crisis Situations.

Rounding out the book, Chapter 20 unveils The Secret Sauce, while Chapters 21 and 22 focus on how to apply persuasion and influence in every aspect of life for lasting success.

This comprehensive guide offers actionable insights for leaders, sales professionals, entrepreneurs, and anyone looking to enhance their influence skills in personal and professional settings.

Jujuvibe Tarot

JujuVibe Tarot: Discover the Mystical World Within
JujuVibe Tarot is not just a Tarot guidebook; it's a journey into the depths of the soul, offering insights and wisdom like never before. This e-book delves into the rich tapestry of the Tarot, providing readers with an immersive experience into the world of understanding others and self-discovery.

Whether you are a beginner or an experienced Tarot enthusiast, JujuVibe Tarot offers something for everyone. Each card in the JujuVibe deck is explored in-depth, with detailed descriptions, symbolism analysis, and practical interpretations that resonate with contemporary life.

Discover the secrets of the Major and Minor Arcana, unlock the mysteries hidden within the symbols, and learn how to conduct your own readings with clarity and confidence. JujuVibe Tarot is more than a guide; it's a companion on your spiritual journey.

Highlights of the book include:

Comprehensive interpretations of the 78 Tarot cards.

Guides to various Tarot spreads for different types of readings.

Insights into the historical and mystical aspects of Tarot.

Practical tips for reading Tarot for personal growth and guidance.

Embark on a path of enlightenment and understanding with JujuVibe Tarot. Your journey towards inner wisdom and self-discovery awaits. Available now on Kindle.

Buddy Loves (Great Day Farm - Children's Book Series 1)

Buddy Loves is a wonderful photographic story of a big, beautiful golden retriever named Buddy. Buddy has a superpower, and his superpower is Love. Buddy loves his family, his tennis balls, swimming, walking, boating, and so much more. Buddy loves completely and unconditionally wit his whole heart and soul. Let buddy into your heart and feel the Love!

Snuggle A Snowflake (Great Day Farm - Children's

Book Series 2)

Snuggle A Snowflake is a wonderful and witty photographic story of a rescue kitten adopted by a lovely family. Snowflake loves to look out of windows, watch out over the front yard, sleep in her cat tree, and boxes, but more than anything else, Snowflake loves to snuggle. She is a snowflake you can snuggle, that will not melt and disappear.
Be advised: The struggle to snuggle is real!

Sleepy Steve (Great Day Farm - Children's Book Series 3)

Steve, the fluffy red tabby kitten, is always sleepy. Watch Steve get comfy and fall asleep all around the house, in all kinds of positions and situations. Steve grows as the book progresses into a full grown, beautiful cat. But make no mistake,
Steve is very sleepy!

Rescue Baybay (Great Day Farm - Children's Book Series 4)

Rescue Baybay is a beautifully photographic story of a small puppy adopted through a rescue at a pet store on a Saturday in September. Baybay goes home with her new family and meets so many new brothers and sisters. However, Baybay has a lot of fear and anxiety that she is not sure how to manage. She barks very loudly when she get worried. Her family reassures her there is nothing to be afraid of. Rescue Baybay is aa wonderful story of love, rescue, and acceptance. through unconditional love and lots of patience, Baybay grows and grows... but she still might have to bark really loudly.

Everyone Loves Dmitri (Great Day Farm - Children's Book Series 5)

Everyone Loves Dmitri is a beautiful photographic story of a rescue kitten. He goes to live with his new family, where he finds new brothers and sisters and friends. Dmitri is a wonderful kitty, who is very anxious at first, but soon settles in to a secure and loving home. He loves to play with his brother, Steve, but he finds himself waiting patiently for Steve to wake up from all of his naps.
Dmitri is so eager to play with anyone and everyone.
It's no wonder that
Everyone Loves Dmitri!

A Dog Named Moose (Great Day Farm - Children's Book Series 6)

A Dog Named Moose - Great Day Farm, Book 6

A Dog Named Moose is a heartwarming photographic journey showcasing the life of a Newfoundland puppy named Moose. This charming tale begins as Moose joins his new family, embarking on an adventure filled with love, growth, and discovery.

Moose quickly grows from a lovable puppy into a giant, gentle dog. He finds joy in the simplest things - his toys, the comfort of a sofa, the refreshing splash of a shower, and most importantly, the love of his family. His story is not just about growing in size; it's about the unbreakable bond he forms with his new brothers, sisters, and friends at Great Day Farm.

Join Moose as he outgrows the sea but never the hearts of those who adore him. Read along as this wonderful puppy teaches us that no matter how big we get, there's always room for unconditional love.